ReFired
NOT **Retired**

RE-IGNITE YOUR ZEST FOR LIFE

by
Phyllis May

**Published by
Wingspan Press**

Published by Wingspan Press
A division of Keys to Paradise, Inc.
1800 Atlantic Blvd.; Key West, FL 33040
http://www.refiredretired.com
http://www.retiredrefired.com
877-312-1800

ISBN: 0-975-8997-1-6

Every effort has been made to determine the source of quotations/cartoons. If brought to the attention of the author/publisher, verified credit for quotations will be attributed in the next printing. Send contributions to info@refiredretired.com.

Visit our website at:
www.refiredretired.com
www.retiredrefired.com

Book design: Ad Graphics, Inc.
Cover/graphics: Jim@JimWeems.com

What does all that mean? It means:

- Don't copy the book; buy it. I'm living on a fixed teachers' retirement and social security. Give me a break!
- I'm not responsible if you don't like my suggestions.
- I'm just trying to adjust your attitude, if that's even necessary, so **we can all enjoy a ReFIRED Life!**

Acknowledgements

Few projects are ever accomplished without the encouragement and support of family, friends, coworkers, business professionals and pets. My endeavors are no different. My daughter, Liane, is the inspiration to model what this time of life can be...and yet I know that her time will be different, just as ours is different from our parents' retirement model.

This and my other book, *Keys to Paradise...a fun guide to Key West* would never have been written had I not had friends and acquaintances from the Florida Speakers Association and the National Speakers Association who not only encouraged me but shared their knowledge in so many different ways.

Special appreciation goes to Jim Barber, who has nagged me for at least five years, as well as Todd Hunt, Sheryl Roush, Sam Horn, Dan Poynter, Dian Thomas, Carolyn Stein, Lisa Bell, Bill Umble, Janet Hayes, Joe Campbell, Dr. Sally Goldberg, Dr. Gayle Carson, Patrick Astre, Glenna Salsbury and Vicki Grant. My daughter and Vicki gave me an ultimatum at my last birthday brunch...." Stop talking and do it!" Don't you love it when you reverse roles with your child/children?

Finally, a special thanks to the new friends I've made. Many of my friends shared their friends when I sent an email to "the world" asking for contributions of their own or asking them to forward my email to others. That process introduced me to a new group of ReFIRED friends around the country. We should someday have a "union"....since it wouldn't be a "re" union!

To all of you...your spirit, your encouragement and your zest will make a difference. You've ignited...keep your fire going and share the message!

Table of Contents

"You saved $126 for your retirement. My advice is
to convert it all to pennies and reinvest it
at the nearest wishing well."

Introduction

After 10 years, I still haven't gotten used to saying "I'm retired." Somehow it's one of those things that most of us think will be in the future and we casually talk about "when I retire, I'm going to…….." But the reality of it is so remote that most of us really don't put ourselves in that picture. It's someone else, but aging, and realizing that we're aging, is something most of us can deflect easily and then…. BAM…it's there! It can't be. It can't be me.

The reality is often mixed emotions. Even if your retirement is planned, there is still concern because it is a new adventure. Like parenting, you learn as you go. Like parenting, you could read, take classes and mentally prepare but when that baby arrives, nothing has prepared you for your emotions. In the case of retirement, little has prepared you for the reality that this is…the rest of your life!

Because retirement today is so much different than retirement in the past, you and I are forging a new path…one unlike the path most of our parents took. In our own way, we're modeling a different path for our children but, by the time they get there, someone else will be writing their book, talking about how they can't follow what their parents modeled to them. And the cycle repeats itself.

The last thing I ever thought I would do is write a book about retiring. Yes, I read about "golden parachutes" but frankly, it had never occurred to me that anything about retirement had changed. And, as I talk to people, I think others are stuck in the old mentality. A few retirees or pre-retirees "get it" but there are so many who haven't realized the possibilities ahead. When I finally realized that nothing was holding me back, the possibilities became endless. In my excitement and enthusiasm, I felt the need to share so that it doesn't take others as long as it took me to catch on.

We have the potential of living longer than previous generations. By taking care of ourselves, along with good genes, someone retiring at 55 has every reason to believe that living to 95 is, for our generation, the rule....not the exception.

Attitude is paramount to making these 20, 30, or 40 years the best years. It will take effort and commitment but I challenge you to make every effort to make your life a ReFIRED life. Adjust your deck chair and join me as the curtain is raised on the second act, giving it our all, for a standing ovation.

I got "high" with my daughter on my 60th birthday!

Part I

Which Way Is Your Deck Chair Facing?

by Charles Schulz

Chapter I

How'd I get to be over the hill when I haven't reached the top?

Mary Phairas lived most of her life in Michigan but at 75, she now lives in Arizona. During "Life, Part I," she paid bills by being a bookkeeper/accountant but she always had an itch to be an entrepreneur. During that part of life, I suspect that many of her businesses were hobbies.

In 2000, Mary Phairas heard about **Crayons to Computers** *and the wonderful success the organization was bringing to the Ohio valley area. With a daughter and granddaughter teaching in the Michigan school system, she knew all too well that Ohio's school budget problems were national in scope. She promised someday to open a similar store for Arizona teachers.*

That promise has now become a reality. In June of 2004, Mary received her federal 501 (c) (3) non-profit certification and signed a lease for 5,000 square feet of retail store space. Today, she and a handful of devoted volunteers are building Arizona's first free store for teachers, called **Treasures 4 Teachers***. Check it out at www.treasures4teachers.org.*

But if you think for one minute that that's her only claim to fame in her "reFIRED" life, think again. Mary has written a book, gone on a booksigning tour with it AND she has created very successful calendars for the Red Hat Society...a great organization for spunky ladies. (www.redhatsociety.com) Mary's book, "The More You Live the Less You Die" is a series of funny anecdotes about her adventures with two of her also spunky friends. All of them have earned Gayle Carson's designation of SOB's... Spunky Old Broads. In spite of Mary's lightheartedness, her greatest satisfaction in her reFIRED life has been the founding of her charity.

Now, at 74, she reminds us of the Energizer Bunny...she just keeps going and going....Her kids are amazed at the things she does since she is busier now than when she worked (for a check).

Mary says, "Now I realize I don't ever intend to quit doing something. I'm just not the retiring kind." Mary is a perfect example of someone who retired from a job but not from life!

MaryPharais
Scottsdale, AZ

Retirement! What a word and what a variety of emotions that word elicits.

Let's not disappoint anyone...a book about retirement needs to start with some dictionary definition of the word so Merriam Webster will do just fine. Here it is: "Retire; verb: conclude one's working or professional career." OK...we all know that but this is us; this is your generation...the generation that redefined "acting your age!" For some, the generation "descriptor" has started with the word BABY. What a shock to have been a part of something described by "baby" for so many years and then suddenly find the word RETIRED close to or after your name. Some have asked the question, "How did I get to be *over the hill* when I'm still trying to reach the top?" Suddenly, "baby" is the wrong descriptor and it's time to get over it!

But, do me a favor! Read that again. "Retire; verb: CONCLUDE ONE'S WORKING OR PROFESSIONAL CAREER." Let me make this point perfectly clear. It is the most important message that you need to hear. It does NOT say that you retire from LIFE. Retiring means you finish your career job. It is NOT the end of anything else. It is the BEGINNING! It is the BEGINNING of a part of life that has the potential to be the most enjoyable, rewarding and satisfying part yet. In Abigail Trafford's book, *My Time: Making the Most of the Rest of Your Life*, she makes the point that "we have a whole new stage in the life cycle, which we haven't had before." [1]

So what is it about retiring or retirement that sometimes causes such anxiety? While I want to avoid some familiar terms, like baby boomer, Steve Slon, the editor of AARP The Magazine, identifies the "boomer gestalt" as a "web of contradictory emotions in which you still feel "with it," yet notice your body responding differently; in which you deny your mortality but can't help growing introspective about the time left to you." Of course there are concerns. It's all new. It's that uncharted territory. How do you view it?

Think about it. Lucy asked Charlie Brown, "Which direction is your deck chair facing?" What about you? Is your deck chair facing the rear of the ship so you can see where you've been or is it facing forward so you can see where you're going?

If Lucy asked you that question, what would your answer be? Are you excited? Are you not going to look back? Are you possibly going to miss some things but not enough to dwell on it? Or, are you worried? Do you wonder what you will do to occupy your time? If you have a spouse who hasn't retired, do you worry about the effect on your relationship?

These are general concerns that could affect anyone but you probably have other issues that are specific to you and your situation. One key is planning. The five years prior to retirement and the five years after are crucial to making this part of your life the "reFIRED" part.

What is a "reFIRED" life? It's all about attitude. It's about being willing to take risks. It's about learning. It's about choices. It's about you!

Having concerns is normal. We're going into our uncharted territory and the possibilities are endless. The important thing is to allow those concerns to surface. If you've got someone you can truly share it with, then do it. If not, putting your thoughts on paper is a good beginning. Once you acknowledge them, they're much easier to deal with.

We've all grown up hearing that there are two things in life that you can count on...death and taxes. For a sizeable number of us, retiring is most certainly the third. Very few escape it and most look forward to it...at least until it begins to close in.

For many years, retiring has been an abstract dream that means no alarm clock, no boss, endless travel, drinks with umbrellas and our own customized wish list. Retiring is that "someday" dream that helps us get through today.

For our parents' generation, the generation modeling retirement to us, it meant travel and golf (if you had money) or often meant boredom (if you didn't).

It's no wonder that statistics show that people who retire and feel no real purpose often die within 17 months. I'm here to tell you that's outrageous and I'm committed to doing whatever it takes in the remaining pages to see that, by the time you close this book, you will make a vow to become one of "our" generation who is "reFIRED, not retired."

It's coming! Embrace the concept and, as trite as it sounds, look at your glass as half full. Life may be good but with your commitment, it can only get better.

We've all heard of a midlife crisis. When my daughter was 25, we became aware of a wonderful book by Alexandra Robbins and Abby Wilner called "The Quarterlife Crisis: The Unique Challenges of Life in Your Twenties." It hit the nail on the head but it also made me begin to think… was there another opportunity for crisis at the other end of life? Now that I've retired and have the opportunity to be a part of this experience, I can definitely answer that question. YES! This can be a crisis time. Finding a name for it isn't so easy…do we call it a ¾ life crisis or a ⅔ life crisis? Maybe we call it your POST midlife crisis. Or do we just call it retirement?

Personally, I've often referred to it as "Life, Part II." The reality is that if you think of the various stages of your life, it could be "Life, Part Seventeen." So, knowing that we have had lots of stages of our life, let's just agree to be consistent and let's refer to this stage of life as "Life, Part II."

Are you beginning to think of possibilities instead of disabilities? Attitude is everything! Your journey is just beginning...not ending.

Now is the time to think not of being retired but reFIRED. What is reFIRED? ReFIRED is committing to spend Life, Part II, focusing on this stage of life. Retirement is like a second childhood. Now, what do you really want to do when you grow up? The possibilities are endless!

Before you go any further, write down five things you'd like to experience during your "reFIREment."

1. _____

2. _____

3. _____

4. _____

5. _____

Keys to ReFIREment

Plan, don't be afraid to take risks, and make choices that lead to a ReFIRED Life!

Chapter 2

You can't turn back the clock but you can wind it up again!

Jane Adams describes her "Lightness of Being" when she moved from her home of 14 years. She tossed the things she couldn't bear to throw out when her parents died. She tossed things from her wedding and tchotchkes and souvenirs from travels. It was hard. Many of us have gone through that process and others know it will need to be done. She describes the difference between "nostalgia and loss"..."One is memory; the other is loss." She relates that she "finally felt a sense of lightness and realized that she was divesting, not downsizing."

According to Adams, "Downsizing is about pinching, restricting and cutting back while keeping yesterday's dreams alive; divesting is about freedom, expansion, redefining the self and dreaming new ones." [1]

At the end of the previous chapter, what kinds of things did you list? Did they involve learning, helping, playing, working or simply enjoying?

Look at the things that are currently occupying your time. How many of those activities are there because they somehow had a job connection? When the job is gone, will you continue with those things? For example, if you bowl in a company bowling league, do you want to continue?

If you're going to begin to phase out, let people know early. If you're in a leadership position in organizations, do what is necessary to help your club with a smooth transition. Sure, it's possible to walk out and burn bridges but why would you?

Begin putting your personal house in order.

We talked earlier about your attitude toward retirement...excitement or anxiety?

People with anxiety often are fearful. This is the time to address those fears. Speak openly, especially to someone who can be helpful, about those fears.

Most of us are not independently wealthy and realize that we are not in the financial position that we should be. All of those years of not wanting to think of retiring have finally caught up. Most pre-retirees who identify "fear" as a concern, generally do so in the context of "fear of finances."

Patty Leeson, an event planner from Kansas City, took a marketing survey about retirement and she said, "It was a big reality check for me. Until then, I had always thought that retirement was down the road and I'd have time to save. But answering those questions made me realize that retirement is like a truck bearing down on me. And I'm not ready." [2]

Growing up and working for years with our parents' retirement model is now often proving to have been a promise that will not be fulfilled. Remember, this is not your daddy's retirement model. In many ways, our generation is in uncharted territory but we're not modeling retirement for our children. It seems apparent that it would be unwise for any Gen XYZer to put much faith in Social Security or company retirement plans. We may be off in uncharted territory but our model probably won't be appropriate for them. All we can do is show them that this period of our life is one to celebrate, to flourish and enjoy the ride to the end. Our children will be challenged as their retirement nears but ours is here.

Our first course of action is to put the wheels in motion to begin to unwind.

Like any clutter, determine what stays and what goes. By clutter, I don't mean to be insensitive or to imply that clutter is negative. I'm just saying that, if you want, you can make this an opportunity to declutter...and I don't mean just *things.*

One night, probably in the 60's, I heard Marlo Thomas say on Johnny Carson, "Today is the first day of the rest of your life." That really resonated. I'd never heard that before and, of course now, everyone has heard that but it is so applicable to the attitude that will serve you well as you look forward to...and ponder...how you're going to spend the rest of your life.

There are, of course, all of the variables in each of our lives. But most of us will hopefully have more freedom, fewer responsibilities, more time at our disposal and CHOICES.

For years, we've had choices but those choices usually revolved around our children, spouse or significant other, pets, parents, jobs and other things that limited our choices.

The strange thing is that often we cling to things, responsibilities or activities because we've done them so long that even if we no longer need to continue, we do. Think about it. Is there anything you continue to do that you could turn over to someone else? For example, did you start teaching Sunday School when your children were little and, even though they have children of their own now, you're still teaching Sunday School? As well intentioned as you might be, did you ever consider that someone actually could fill your shoes and that, if you weren't there, the sky wouldn't fall? Do you ever consider that maybe they need new blood and, more importantly, that YOU need something new?

If you downsize or divest, as Jane Adams did, and you begin to see things as she sees them, you understand that a lot of this is about change and change is often difficult. It's much more comfortable to stay in the rut we're in but I beg you…open yourself to change. If you don't…or won't…you might as well stop reading. This book isn't for you. Becoming reFIRED is a process, an attitude and a commitment to make the most of this wonderful new era of our life.

Keys to ReFIREment

- **Being willing and flexible enough to change is paramount to your success.**
- **Put your personal "house" in order!**

Chapter 3

Is it time to plant your peach tree?

Dr. Robert Olson is a cardiologist who bought an old farm house in France. He visits there every July and has spent several years making it more inhabitable and planting his garden. He says, "It's still just an old farm house." This year, the peach tree next door bore fruit shortly after he left. His French neighbor sent him lots of peach conserve, made from the fruit, so he could enjoy it as if he were there. I asked him if it was in his plan to retire to France at some point and this was his reply.... "I would love that but I realize I need to plant my peach tree soon."

What will be the "peach tree" in your retired life? If you haven't retired yet, what seeds need to be sown now to be ready for your enjoyment when you do retire? And, if you have retired, it's still not too late. Our "life after work" period has the potential to last approximately 30 years so don't say it's too late because you haven't done it. But planning is always helpful.

All of us know that throughout life we've often had opportunities to make mistakes and learn from them. For example, a first marriage might be considered a "dress rehearsal" for a successful one to follow. We've all had experiences where we know what didn't work, correct it and succeed the next time.

Retirement, however, often doesn't afford the same opportunities. Most of us only retire once and there aren't as many years on the back end to clean up bad decisions or lack of preparation. Therefore, retirement often comes without

Dr. Olson's farm house in France.

Peach tree near Dr. Olson's French home.

a dress rehearsal for this second act. Getting it right often saves *time* and *money*. At this stage, those two elements are two of our most valued. Investing wisely in both will bring much needed dividends to our reFIRED life.

If we did have the luxury of dress rehearsal, what would you include?

1.

2.

3.

4.

5.

Thinking of these things ahead of time begins the process of prioritizing and it helps with the often difficult task mentioned earlier...decluttering.

Many of us come from "full steam ahead" to "no steam" overnight. Most of us don't know the answers to much when it comes to retirement but there is help available. Planning can make the transition much better and there are organizations which can help you. Here are some resources that can get you started.

Bernice Bratter, 68, of Westwood Hills, California, retired once and "losing her sense of identity as well as the stimulation, daily responsibilities and social interactions of her job left her listless and depressed." She says emphatically, "Well, it was a disaster!" Eventually, she returned to work, but this time she planned ahead for her re-retirement. She gathered 10 professional women together to discuss retirement transition and life planning. The women called their venture *Project Re-*

newment. They trademarked the name, intending to produce a manual someday to help others replicate their group.

Civic Ventures is a nonprofit in San Francisco that encourages older adults to remain active citizens. Their director, Marc Freedman, says that "there are plenty of opportunities to do financial planning for retirement, but when it comes to figuring out a period of life that's as long as midlife in duration, you're on your own." (www.civicventures.org)

Many communities and community colleges have created their own programs. One of the most comprehensive is in the town of Chandler, Arizona. Their "Boomerang" program provides a variety of resources. The coordinator, Linda Meissner, says, "Boomers don't see retirement as freedom from work but as freedom to choose what's next." (www.myboomerang.org)

Copyright 2004 by Randy Glasbergen.
www.glasbergen.com

**Investments and
Financial Planning**

"If you want to retire someday, you'll need a quadruple bypass: bypass the sports car dealership, bypass the jewelry store, bypass the travel agency, and bypass the betting parlor!"

The Transition Network (TTN) was formed in New York City six years ago and chapters are now being formed in other locations. There are more than 2500 women, mostly in their fifties and sixties, who represent a spectrum of professions and believe that the strength in networking is vital as they make life transitions. The website lists where additional chapters have been formed and tells how to form your own chapter in your locale. (www.thetransitionnetwork.org)

There are lots of resources available to provide assistance, networking, mentoring, coaching and support for your wonderful life ahead. There are few major events in life that you don't plan for. It's time to get serious if you haven't already. Don't be afraid to ask for directions. Central Florida Community College has developed a series called Pathways to Living, Learning and Serving. Trained volunteer coaches, most of whom are retirees, coach 55+ adults on "creating a road map for the rest of their lives." (www.pathwaysmarion.com) [1]

With no dress rehearsal, realistic planning is imperative and will help make Life, Part II, the part that ends with the standing ovation from your friends and family who have witnessed the life you led.

Keys to ReFIREment

Plan...but plan realistically!

Chapter 4
Be your own navigator!

"After raising a family and teaching for many years, Marian Ross Hall retired (from that life). At the age of 67, she registered at Indiana University as a special student in the Slavic Department, and started systematically taking four years of Russian language courses. Despite her status as a special student, she took all the examinations, wrote all the term papers and made virtually a straight A record. When she had completed the equivalent of an undergraduate major in Russian, she made practical use of her language by taking time out one summer for a tour of Russia... all without fanfare, in her usual unassuming way.

After her return, she started taking graduate courses in Russian literature – still for credit, writing all the required term papers, taking all the examinations, and making A's on every one of them. She went through almost enough graduate courses to have earned another master's degree.

As chairman of the Slavic department at that time, I tried in vain to persuade her to let the Indiana University News Bureau publish an article about the adventurous way she was spending her retirement, but she wouldn't hear of it. Her refusal caused me deep frustration. I FELT A SOCIAL OBLIGATION TO REMIND THE WORLD THAT RETIREMENT DOES NOT HAVE TO MEAN WATCHING TV ALL DAY OR EVEN DOZING IN THE FLORIDA SUN, PLEASANT AS THAT MAY BE.

Marian Ross Hall died in 1998 at the age of 95 which frees me now to tell the remarkable story of what she did with her life."[1]

William Edgerton
Indiana University, Professor Emeritus
Slavic Languages and Literatures

Marian Ross Hall took charge and exemplifies the kind of life that can occur. For 28 years after her decision to pursue her interest in Slavic languages, Marian embarked on a new and different path. But, in order to do it, she had to take charge. She made choices in an earlier part of her life, choices that I'm sure she never regretted. However, when she had the opportunity to make choices to accomplish some things she'd never had the time to do…she did it. She didn't think…"I'm too old" or "what's the point?" She thought of possibilities…not disabilities.

What makes "taking charge" possible and why is it important? For most of our pre-Life, Part II lives, we may or may not have been in control. I suspect that many of us were in control and had pride in ourselves because we were, or felt we were, in charge.

I also suspect that there are just as many who never felt in control. In many cases, these people were not in control simply because of their responsibility to others or a job. They might have appeared to be strong on the surface but a strong exterior often simply means that they function effectively yet may still be at the mercy of other people or things. Most of us go through many years in this mode. Being a strong person, able to juggle many things, is precisely the reason they may have little control over their own lives.

There are also those who are very dependent and truly don't have the skills or the mindset to be in control of their lives. It would be unusual if these people are interested in becoming reFIRED since a reFIRED life involves a certain amount of independence and risk.

Being your own navigator...taking charge of your own destiny...seems quite obvious but it is hard to think selfishly when most of our adult lives have revolved around other people. Spouses, parents, children, pets and the job have not usually allowed us to make decisions in which the outcome of the decision centered as much only on us.

Allow yourself this luxury. Allow yourself to make decisions that are more self-centered than you're probably used to. It's one of the hardest habits to break but you've got to start somewhere...and sometime...if you're going to allow yourself to participate in Life, Part II, to the fullest advantage.

Stephen Schwartz' song, "No Time at All," from Pippin shouts at us, telling us:

"It's time to start livin',
Time to take a little from this world we're given."

That time is now. It is time to START livin'. Look back at your life...pre Life, Part II. Life is about choices and the choices that created your adult life until the choices which come with retirement.

Previous choices probably limited your freedom as years went along. Whether you married or had a significant relationship...that's the relationship that often began the series of choices that, even in the best of situations, began to slowly make our own destiny more complicated. Children, parents, pets, jobs, bills and other individual responsibilities have combined or accumulated in such a way that our choices often are limited. That is not a bad thing and most of us wouldn't want it any other way. In the "leadership" world, we talk about *servant leadership*. The reality is that most responsible adults have lived as *servant leaders* in their families. It always involved choices and usually choices which put everyone else before us.

Because of that, taking charge of your own destiny might be one of the hardest tasks you have, if you'd like for Life, Part II to be a reFIRED life.

After many years of being responsible to and for others, it might take therapy for us to allow ourselves to be a little selfish with our decision for enjoying Life, Part II, to the fullest.

They say, "Freedom is when the kids leave home and the dog dies." You can add your variation to that but it's something to think about. How can you rewrite that to apply to you? MY freedom is when ⎯⎯⎯⎯⎯⎯⎯⎯⎯⎯⎯⎯⎯

⎯⎯⎯⎯⎯⎯⎯⎯⎯⎯⎯⎯⎯⎯⎯⎯⎯⎯⎯⎯⎯⎯⎯⎯⎯⎯⎯⎯⎯

⎯⎯⎯⎯⎯⎯⎯⎯⎯⎯⎯⎯⎯⎯⎯⎯⎯⎯⎯⎯⎯⎯⎯⎯⎯⎯⎯⎯⎯

What are the limiting factors that keep you from being free enough to determine your own destiny? Let me say it another way…if you would like Life, Part II, to be a reFIRED life, what is preventing you from doing it? Hopefully there aren't many but if there's even one, you have to deal with it. List your limiting factors below:

1. _____

2. _____

3. _____

4. _____

5. _____

Now, think through the possible solutions. Are they really the obstacles you think or is it your PRE Life, Part II, mentality still kicking in when it no longer needs to.

"I think I have enough money for a comfortable retirement. All I need to be comfortable is a pair of soft slippers and some loose underwear."

That mentality will now become baggage if you continue to carry it. Tossing any of your baggage in life is a very difficult task but successfully minimizing it has to be the beginning of getting to a reFIRED life. Decide right now that you are going to do whatever is necessary to minimize regrets. This is the time. If you've always wanted to learn to play the banjo, then stop talking about it and do it.

Take a few minutes and write below a solution word or phrase corresponding to the limiting factors you listed previously:

1. _____

2. _____

3. _____

4. _____

5. _____

Keys to ReFIREment

**Take charge of your own destiny...
be your own navigator...both keys to
a reFIRED life! What's stopping you?**

Chapter 5

What's your destination?

Having been a teacher for 36 years, Fran Bell Simms of Arlington, VA, made sure that the first year that school opened after she retired, she wasn't around. She didn't want to feel obligated to chase the yellow school buses down the street.

Fran had always been passionate about art...both creating it and admiring it... so when the school opened, she went to the south of Ireland to a watercolor workshop. With a friend, "whose parents had come from the old sod," they visited Limerick and spent time in their home as an additional treat. She became the "wandering taster of fish chowder" since everyone along the coast of Ireland makes it fresh with the catch of the day.

After that inspiring trip, early in her retirement, she has persisted with watercolor, now teaches adults in the evening and has become a member of two art leagues which exhibit and sell. She says, "I have always been passionate about art and seeing it: NOW I have added being passionate about making it and passing that on to others."

ADVICE: *"If you cannot do it joyfully, don't do it at all."*

Most of us are very linear in our thinking and planning. We learned to outline at an early age and even if we don't formally sit down and make an outline, we usually look at long range plans in logical steps. I suggest that you **not** follow that method in preparing for your reFIRED life. Instead, identify "the end" with space between where you are and where you want to be and then....work backwards. (I want to make it perfectly clear that "the end" doesn't mean.... "the end." We really don't have to plan on that "end!")

With life expectancies for baby boomers projected to be in the 90's, you can see why these years are a significant part of our total time on earth. When life expectancy was much shorter, there truly wasn't much time between a normal retirement at 65 and death. Health issues were often not able to be resolved and many people were genuinely worn out.

Two interesting websites for the 50+ group...a group that is growing by 8,000 people per day...are www.livingto100. com and www.eons.com. The first website, which is Dr. Thomas Perls', links to the second. One of the most popular features, accessible at both, is their Longevity Calculator, which, by the way, tells me that I will live to be 95. Take it just for curiosity without putting any faith into the results. The idea, according to its developer, Dr. Perls, is to get the attention of the group checking it out.

The Life Expectancy Calculator considers important determinants of longevity. After taking it, you will receive a personalized report that provides you with specific steps you can take to increase your longevity. You will also receive a personalized "to-do" list to take to your doctor, which includes questions to ask, plus examinations, tests, and vaccinations you should have. [1]

When Dr. Perls was interviewed by Daniel Kadlec, author of *The Power Years: A User's Guide to the Rest of Your Life*, Perls says that people "are amazed to see that they will live 20 years longer than their great-grandparents and with less illness at the end of their life."

Kadlec feels "it's about time someone found a way to drive that point home." He feels that although there are many resources to help, it's a hard point to drive home about "how the longer, healthier lives of boomers will change the game. There's something sobering about a 10-minute quiz that finds your life, at 50, is barely half over. Do I have enough savings? Should I work longer? Start a business? **How can I make my next 50 years count?**" [2]

If you look at our lives now, you could say that the first 50-60 years are for growing up, and for most people, committed to family and jobs. This second part is now often the part that can provide us, in its own way, a very unique kind of satisfaction. What we call it, doesn't matter. It is our reFIRED Life...a life segment based on our maturity, our experiences, our relationships and our will to live a very significant part of our life to the fullest.

Get started now...identify the end that you have in mind. Visualize, if necessary, your realistic, possible life. Go one step beyond visualizing it...write it down and describe it. In fact, go to the next page and do it right now.

During my refired life, I would like to:

1. _____

2. _____

3. _____

4. _____

5. _____

Hints or suggestions for goals might be: [3]

- Travel to ....
- Learn to speak ....
- Lose .... Pounds
- Volunteer at ....
- Learn to ....
- Cruise to ....
- Buy a ....
- _____ with my family
- Start _____ing again
- Dare
  to ....

www.eons.com gives you a place for 10 goals and the resources to go with them!

The earlier you start, the more likely you are to reach that visualized end. Some goals might only be accomplished with a certain financial commitment while others might involve specific training or education. There are "end" outcomes that mean relocating, downsizing or rightsizing. Some will involve physical training to accomplish our "end goals." Whatever it takes, the point is that you should identify your visual lifestyle and begin taking the steps to reach it. Having identified "the end," now work backward to determine the actions or steps you need to start with to ultimately get to your target. Begin with the end in mind and work backward but the most important word is this:

BEGIN

How do you begin? First you identify what you think you want to accomplish. The website mentioned above, Eons, has a great place for writing down your goals. When you do, it tells you how many other people have mentioned that as a goal and if any of them live close to you. (You register with a zip code.) In addition, it gives you web resources to find out more about each goal so even if it's something you know nothing about, it gets you started. You can do it yourself in the space I've provided or you can do it more "formally" at a website like Eons. The important thing is to do it.

Another thing to keep in mind is balance in your life. Again, the Eons website discusses the importance of balance. Sometimes this needs to be a conscious effort. Eons shows a pie chart and explains: "It doesn't have to mean an evenly sliced pie of categories. Instead, a balanced life reflects goals that are aligned with your personal values. It's far too easy to focus on the things we think other people will want us to do, or that we think we're supposed to do at this age." [4]

Guy Kawasaki suggests that "if you let the world put you into a role, you never will go beyond that role. Create your own definition of who you are and what you can accomplish."

You begin by remembering that you're never too old. According to Victor Parachin:

"Attitude is ageless. Our attitudes can determine whether we will go forward or retreat, continue or quit, remain open to new opportunities or remain frozen in the past. To achieve success, whatever your age, begin by remembering you're never too old to succeed. History is filled with 'old' people who accomplished great things. Be true to your highest aspirations. Faithfully follow your dreams. Doing so will ensure that you maximize your opportunities and minimize your obstacles." [5]

Remember, also, that "old" should have a new and different meaning to you. Remember when we thought 30 was old...until we got there? And then 40? At age 80, Marv Levy was named General Manager of the NFL's Buffalo Bills. When asked about that appointment at his age, he replied, "The age factor means nothing to me. I'm old enough to know my limitations and I'm young enough to exceed them!"

Keep your destination in mind. Where are you now? What will it take to get you to that point, knowing your limitations? Again, the key word....

Keys to ReFIREment

BEGIN!

Chapter 6

Who knows
where or when?

"My parents didn't want to move to Florida,
but they turned sixty and that's the law."
— Jerry Seinfeld

*I can share my own story for "where" and "when"
since both have been major decisions...as they are
for most of us.*

*I never planned to retire at 55. I loved my 34 years
in education and often said "if I won the lottery, I
wouldn't quit work." I also often said that "retirement might be fun for about two weeks but then I'd
be bored." I'm still waiting for that to happen. When
the opportunity presented itself to retire about 10
years earlier than I ever anticipated, I thought long
and hard. The "when" had presented itself and no,
financially, I wasn't close to being prepared. The
troubling question is this...10 years later would I
have been any better prepared? I sincerely doubt it. I
always thought that my teachers' retirement and Social Security would cover me quite adequately. That
was certainly a false sense of security. The opportunities were there to continue in education but the
overriding factors in the decision to go ahead and
retire was being able to continue with a group health
insurance policy. I had cancer in 1989. I didn't want
to ever lose my insurance and have to look for an
individual policy. Having said that, even on a group
policy, my payments this year are $550/month...much
more than I ever anticipated.*

The "where" is another, more interesting, story. My husband and I had lived in Jacksonville, FL, for 25 years. It was a great place to live and raise our child but I had grown up with my parents' obsession to live in Florida. I never felt like Jacksonville was the "real" Florida. Our family had always had access to my family's condo on Ft. Myers Beach and I think both of us thought that retiring there sometime would be in our future.

By the time I retired, our 20 year marriage had ended. I spent a year, thinking. One day I woke up with a great revelation...my marriage was over, our daughter was away at college, I had just put my mother in an assisted living facility in Michigan and I had to put my dog to sleep. As I mentioned before, they say, "freedom is when the dog dies and the kids leave home." I could add my own variation of that but it suddenly hit me that I didn't have to stay there anymore. There was not a single reason to stay.

I packed some luggage and went to Fort Myers Beach, thinking I would be making some major moving decisions on that trip. After a few days, I decided to drive on down to Key West. Other than occasional trips there as a child, I had no connection to Key West, barely remembered anything about it and the only person I barely knew was on a year long trip around the United States and to Alaska, in a camper. I stayed one night, drove back to Ft. Myers Beach, packed my things, drove to Jacksonville and told everyone that I was moving to Key West. I had no plan. I was 55, alone and moved to a new location to begin my new life. (I told people, who already thought I was a little nuts, that I was going to sell kites on the beach or rent scooters. By then, they probably thought I was wacko enough to do that.)

Key West is a wonderful little town. I know more people in 8 years than I ever knew in 25 years in my former life. It is, without a doubt, the best decision I ever made. While I love Ft. Myers and Ft. Myers Beach, it has gotten to be big. I never would have known as many people as I know in such a short period of time. When you have a job and are in a new city, your initial acquaintances often start with your job colleagues. When you have no job and know no one and are no spring chicken, a small town might work best. It has for me.

*On March 1 of 1998 I left Jacksonville for my new adventure. Because of the significance of March 1, I have designated March 1 of every year as **reFIRED, not Retired Day**. It has been an official day in Chase's Calendar of Events for several years now.*

The big decisions involve the two "W" words..."where" and "when." The one that you might have the least control over is the WHEN. For many, the WHEN probably involves company policies, years of work, age, Social Security and other obligations. Those are the decisions that need forethought. I had always thought I would retire at 65 but instead unexpected circumstances caused me to retire at 55. (According to AARP, 40% of us do retire unexpectedly. The reasons often are due to job loss or health.) Because I never thought that would be an option, I wasn't prepared in any way. It took me a while to decide "what I wanted to be when I grew up"...at age 55...but it was also a wonderful surprise. We can't all plan, as I'm suggesting, but speaking from experience, things will probably go more smoothly if you "do as I say, not as I did!"

WHEN, therefore, should be factored in as part of your plan. If, for whatever reason, your WHEN changes, you, at least, have a plan. If you have to modify that plan, so be it. It's easier to modify than it is to be caught off guard with no plan, when you're in a state of shock anyway. My suggestion: Once you turn 50, if you haven't already, get started putting things in writing. I've given you some opportunities already. Thinking about things or visualizing is a good first step but committing something to writing gives it a sense of reality. It can always be changed but your plan starts with WHEN.

The KEY is to be *realistic* with your plan. A recent study by the Employee Benefits Research Institute indicated that people currently working think that they can get by with 70% of their income. On the other hand, 66% of people who have already retired have found that 70% isn't enough.

Financial responsibility for retirement is, more often than not, in the hands of the individual but most of us started our working years with the idea that Social Security and company pensions would take care of us. As we've gotten older we've seen company after company renege on their responsibility to employees and, in many cases, leave them with nothing. If you haven't retired yet, you simply must realistically look at your anticipated post-retirement finances. There are many sources for calculating what you will need to retire on. No matter how young you are, you will be better prepared when you make that calculation. That's an important first step and that step will help you accomplish what was said previously.

BE REALISTIC!

Another factor involved with the WHEN might be our spouse or significant other. "Couples tend to retire at the same time, which isn't surprising," says Sandra Block of

"We can afford to retire in 20 years, but only if our credit cards retire in 10 years."

USA Today. "If you want to travel in retirement, after all, it's nice to have company." In a major change of life like this, it's best to "synchronize" with your partner. Block mentions that "most of us think of retirement as an end to the everyday hassles of the working world. But if you and your partner have different plans and goals, retirement could turn out to be even more stressful than work." [1]

"Joint retirement can create financial problems for women," says Alicia Munnell, director of the Center for Retirement Research at Boston College.

Along those lines, Block cautions that the average wife is three years younger than her husband, and women typically live longer than men. And Munnell advises that "while men like having company in retirement, I think women need to be a little selfish." [2]

WHERE, on the other hand, can have endless possibilities...or none. None if you have been in the same place for years, live close to your parents or children/grandchildren and wouldn't consider being far away.

ENDLESS if you feel like this is your time to make choices of your own. For some people, it can never happen. They're happy and wouldn't have it any other way.

For others, the chosen destination might have been a previous vacation spot, a location close to other interests or might simply have to do with climate or cost of living.

Block says that "despite a boom in retirement communities, most couples don't move when they retire." Yet Amy Noel, a financial planner in Boulder, Colorado, says "many

GOT SOME QUESTIONS?
ANSWERS AVAILABLE [3]

Even if you're still in your 20s, it's not too early to start talking about retirement with your spouse. Use this checklist, developed by the AARP and USA TODAY, to gauge your retirement compatibility.

Question	Where to get more information
At what age do you plan to retire?	www3.troweprice.com/ric/RIC/
At what age do you expect to start drawing Social Security benefits?	www.ssa.gov/planners/calculators.htm
How much do you expect to get from Social Security?	www.ssa.gov/planners/calculators.htm
Where do you want to live after you retire?	www.aarpmagazine.org/lifestyle/dream_towns.html
What are your travel plans in retirement?	www.elderhostel.org/
Do you plan to work part time in retirement?	www.aarp.org/money/careers/

of her married clients agree that they want to move when they retire but disagree on where." She says, "If you keep exploring, you'll find something that you both agree on." [4]

Unless you're independently wealthy, cost of living should be a major consideration in your research on places to relocate. Again, I found that out the hard way. I moved to a place with a very high cost of living. I love it and have no regrets but I could be getting a lot more "bang for my retirement buck" in another location. (In another location, however, I wouldn't be writing this with a view of the Atlantic Ocean and an occasional cruise ship passing by.) Oceans, mountains, corn fields, deserts, golf courses… what environment gives you pleasure? If it's your current home, congratulations! You've got one less major decision to make. But, if it's the time to make a move, begin the process or the plan. When the time comes, there shouldn't be surprises if you've done your homework. Home IS where the heart is. Pulling up stakes at midlife is a gutsy thing to do. It's one of the risks that goes with a reFIRED life but a new place, new friends, new activities, new networks…all have the potential for truly helping to create your new reFIRED life.

In the past, the trend has been to move away from big cities. Yet in more recent years, that trend is changing. Opportunities abound in large cities for special interests and entertainment and accessible public transportation is usually easily available.

College and university towns are also places that have gained new interest because of the opportunities that are available and moving out of the country is an option being exercised by many. Because of the inexpensive cost of living, Central America might be a consideration. However, in a foreign country, there are safety issues that should be investigated. Many of these countries are offering incentives to Americans to retire there. Besides the fact that real estate is inexpensive, discounted health care is one of the perks.

Before you decide, ask the questions and determine the realistic answers...especially if it involves someone else. What are the things important to you...weather, availability of health care and the quality of it, culture, cost-of-living and safety? Transportation has been mentioned and how important is it to live close to your children, grandchildren or parents?

Sometimes the decision might be whether to move to a "retirement community." That decision might come up whether you stay in your own area or move to a new one. Just like this whole process of retirement is not your daddy's retirement model, communities for seniors have changed as well. Those that have changed along with their residents should be called "reFIREment communities" but regardless of what they are called, they are changing. As one home-builder in Atlanta told AARP, "they're no longer playing shuffleboard, they're skydiving." If a senior community is in your plans, make sure you find one that meets your needs. As a reFIRED senior, don't get stuck in one where people have moved in and are waiting to die.

This point was brought home to me by my Mother, who spent the last seven years of her life in a wonderful assisted living facility near Detroit. She enjoyed it immensely and took part in most of the events that were planned but many of the residents did nothing but complain. I called her several times a week and during one conversation she said, "I had the most wonderful thought last night. I realized that most of these people came here to die. I came here to live." How profound that was to me and to her! Her attitude was reflected in how she ended up her life…in stark contrast to most of the other "inmates," as she called them, who were just there to pass the time. She would have nothing of that mentality. While we're not talking about assisted living yet, the revelation holds true in whatever stage you are in. Make your choice and go there to LIVE!

If you do decide to stay in your current environment, you can still create a reFIRED life by getting involved in new organizations and perhaps making new acquaintances.

"I can't afford to retire on my planet, so I'm exploring other options."

While teaching leadership skills, specifically teamwork, we emphasize a concept that many people fail to recognize: the addition of one new team member creates a brand new team. In other words, the dynamics of the group is now different with only one change.

The same concept can be said about making new acquaintances or getting involved in new interests. You're now changing your own dynamic somewhat. Just be aware of the change in dynamics, subtle as it may be, so that you're not blindsided by your family or friends who might resent your new activities. A little piece of the puzzle has now been altered and sometimes others feel threatened or are resentful.

Do what you can to lay the groundwork for your reFIRED life and get the support from those who are important in your life to succeed in this challenge.

Remember, living a reFIRED life has nothing to do with money; it has everything to do with attitude! Forty-eight percent of people interviewed said that money is not the key to a satisfying retirement; it's good health.

Getting rid of stress is a key to maintaining that good health and a study at the University of California, San Francisco, recently proved what we all feel like we've known...Stress ages you. Sarah Mahoney interviewed 10 people over 85 and asked for their secrets for eliminating stress. Their responses were:

- Games
- Humor

- Optimism
- Work
- Close relationships
- Altruism
- Music
- Prayer
- Exercise [5]

Keys to ReFIREment

**Great genes help but taking care
of yourself along with a great attitude
can do wonders for your health...
mental and physical.**

Part II

The Curtain Rises!
The Second Act Begins!

Chapter 7

It's here; now what?

In our family, the first day of school each year was a big event. For me, as a child, and for my daughter, we had a new outfit, new school supplies and the photo op for the first day of that grade. The night before the first day of 7th grade, I went to tuck my daughter into bed. Her excitement about the day to come was obvious and she said, "Do you realize I've waited my entire life to be in junior high?"

I suspect that you could say the same thing about retirement..."I've waited my entire life to retire!" Well, now it's all official. The day arrives. There's no alarm clock but chances are, as aggravating as you might find it, you'll wake up early...probably earlier than you want to. This day is ahead of you...and many more to come.

It's only fitting to have mixed emotions at this time...a sense of freedom and a sense that you should be doing something at work. Actually letting go might be harder than you think it will be because we're so excited. We think there will be no adjustment. Most people have a little more problem than they anticipate but most people also adapt and move ahead quickly.

In the beginning, it's common, expected and normal to treat your initial jobless time as vacation days, doing the things you like and enjoy that are not work related. Then you get to the point where you realize that this is the way your life schedule is going to be for many years. At that point, many people begin to seriously consider how they are going to fill those days and remain mentally and physically healthy and balanced. This isn't a short vacation. This is the rest of your new life...Life, Part II.

What am I going to do now? (Does that remind you of family trips and the persistent question, "When are we going to get there?" Dr. Robert Lopatin reflects that the way "What am I going to do now?" is asked is very telling. Do you understand what he's saying? You can hear it in the pathetic or pitiful voice of someone who is simply lost in knowing what the future holds. You hear it in the voice of someone who hasn't realized that there is enormous freedom in not having constraints.

On the other hand, can you hear the way another person asks the question? "WHAT am I going to do now?" spoken with passion and the feelings of someone anxiously looking for a way to a reFIRED life. Dr. Lopatin relates it to "a second flowering." (Read Dr. Lopatin's story in Chapter 10.)

Aaron Bacall of Staten Island, NY, said that his reaction to retirement was exactly that....what am I going to do now? In Bacall's previous life he had been a chemist as well as a high school teacher and college instructor. He's now been retired 11 years and says he never gives advice but he does suggest that you "address what you felt towards an avocation as a young person." He says that now he's closer to his wife and "I became a calmer, better, more pleasant and more understanding person. The most important part of retirement, and doing what I am interested in, is the loss of job-related stress."

But you'll never guess what this former chemist is doing now...he's writing humor professionally for corporations and having the time of his life. Three of his cartoons have been added to the permanent collection in the Baker Library of the Harvard Business School and he has completed his 5th book of Educational Cartoons, published by Corwin Press. As he pored over those vials, do you think he ever seriously thought that his life would take this turn? I doubt it but these events can happen when you have a passion about something and then pursue it without thinking of all the reasons why it won't happen.

We all know that our physical health is directly related to our mental health. Unfortunately for some, while this time should be a time filled with opportunities, it becomes a time which is "ripe" for depression. People whose identities are strongly tied to their job suddenly don't have that. There are, of course, exceptions with high visibility jobs and the people identified with them. The automatic association of Bill Gates and Microsoft will always exist no matter what Bill Gates is doing. But for those of us in the real world, our job and our "life" were usually intricately connected. The feeling of importance, of feeling valued and a sense of purpose is not easy to suddenly be without. Being able to handle this immediate aspect of retirement is crucial to having and maintaining a healthy mental state. Letting go of your past life and looking forward to possibilities is a key to a mentally healthy reFIRED life.

The aspect of life that is the one which will "get us in the end" is our physical health and our goal should be to do our part, as much as possible, to remain healthy for as long as we can. I know we realize that "stuff" happens and the healthiest people sometimes die or become infirm at an earlier than expected age. On the other side of the coin, some of the hardest living, "abuse the body worst," people live to ripe old ages. Go figure!

In the end, there are things out of our control; things that make our best laid plans obsolete.

There's no question that the remainder of our life, and how it ultimately finishes, is one big question mark. Life is a mystery and a series of surprises.

Along the way there will be setbacks. There usually are and this time is no different. How we deal with these setbacks is crucial. Dr. Alan Loy McGinnis, a corporate consultant and author, interviewed more than 190 women and men to find out why some ordinary people often seem to achieve so much more than others. He discovered that a common trait of high achievers is the ability to bounce back from defeat.

Victor Parachin suggests that you never allow a setback to disrupt your plans and goals. Remind yourself that life is not a straight-line pattern moving you from success to success. Rather, life is often two steps forward and one step back. Bounce back whenever you experience a difficulty or defeat.

Parachin also suggests that maintaining a sense of humor is paramount when things don't work out the way we expect and life becomes discouraging. The ability to laugh at yourself and your circumstances ensures that you are not taking yourself too seriously. Also humor pushes back feelings of depression and discouragement, making room for creativity and commitment. [1]

Until now, for better or for worse, there are things in our life that haven't gone as planned. Yet the planned and the unplanned events have intertwined to create our life...good or bad...warts and all.

It's up to each of us now to do our part to stay healthy, both physically and mentally. Both are keys to living a re-FIRED life. How we fill this time and live these days is directly related to the state of our mental and physical well-being.

Remember, you're retired from your job...not from life!

Keys to ReFIREment

- **Letting go of your past life and looking forward to possibilities is a key to a mentally healthy reFIRED life.**

- **Maintain a sense of humor!**

- **Do your part to stay healthy, both physically and mentally.**

Chapter 8

What's important in your day?

*Andy and Doris Beaumont have lived in Fort Lauder-
dale, Florida, for 45 years...he was an exterminator
and she was in the insurance business. Andy was
semi-retired for 2 ½ years and "controlled everything at home," according to Doris. During their
work lives, they didn't spend much time with non-
profits; like many of us, they were too busy working
while raising their son and daughter.*

*Initially, Doris did work at paid jobs. Between jobs she
did what I did and worked at a temp agency...in her
case, Kelly Girls. I agree with Doris that being a temp
is a very enjoyable job...you choose when you want to
work and meet lots of great people. And, we both had
the same experience that most places we worked were
interested in hiring us full time. They were delighted
to have people who could spell, file and bring a great
work ethic to the job...even if we were only temps.*

*Eventually she got a job for a hydraulic supply com-
pany that supplied the arm of a gorilla at Disney as
well as the earthquake effects. Do you think she ever
thought, during an earlier part of her life, that she
would ever be doing something like this?*

*One day, however, she was scanning the volunteer
ads and noticed that the Red Cross was looking for
someone to do general office work such as typing,
switchboard, front desk, etc. It sounded like fun! She
had never done anything for the Red Cross before
and didn't make the call because of her interest with*

that organization...it simply sounded like a job she could be suited for.

She got the job but then it became more than a routine office job. The Red Cross spirit began to connect. She realized that she wanted to be more involved. She began taking the required courses that Red Cross offers to its volunteers and helped out by answering numerous telephone calls in 1999 when Hurricane Irene hit her area. She was hooked.

But, hold on...Andy couldn't see it. "Why are you spending so much time there and why do you find it so enjoyable? What do you want to do that for," he often asked. Her reply was always, "Why don't you come along?" Andy, being Andy, wanted no part of it. Maybe she eventually wore him down but in a weak moment, he decided to go with her on one of her emergency calls. From that first experience, Andy was hooked.

Andy is 80 and has now taken 8 of the required classes; Doris has taken 9. They're on call 7 days a week, 12 hours a day to assist people with shelter, food, clothing and shoes during emergencies. There are many situations they will never forget and they know that helping people is now their mission.

Andy and Doris have received recognition from the Governor, the Red Cross and their local NBC affiliate chose them for their "Spirit of South Florida" honor.

While Andy was hard to win over, he is definitely a believer now but they both say they wouldn't be able to do it without the support of the other.

Doris says, "Volunteer for something you think you would enjoy and like to do. You never know what it will lead to. I wonder how we ever didn't have volunteering as a priority in our day."

Would you like to know the best thing about my day? No alarm clock! The occasional times that I have to make sure I get up on time just annoy me but they're rare. A 'natural rising' is such a peaceful way to start any day. It's another part of the freedom that you now have.

I can remember many, many nights when I woke up in the middle of the night and couldn't go back to sleep. I got so agitated as I looked at the clock at 4 AM, knowing full well that if I did happen to finally go back to sleep that the alarm would be going off at 5 AM. That makes the day start wrong.

I naturally get up early although I try to discipline myself and MAKE MYSELF stay in bed until 6. It doesn't always work. Sometimes I get up and read the paper in bed and go back to sleep. As amazing a feat as it is for me, then maybe I don't wake up again until 8. Voilá! Who cares? I might have some kind of schedule during the day (later) but not having a forced, unnatural waking is just the best way to start a day!

But what are the important things in your day? Is it exercise, church, reading, crafting, watching TV, socializing, volunteering? What are your priorities?

One of the things that will help get us into our new life is a little bit of a daily routine. You're heading for severe depression if you don't get up every morning and get cleaned up. If you're alone, personal neglect is an easy trap to fall into.

Building exercise into your day should also be a priority and this is more important now than perhaps it ever has been. If you're not into exercise, please don't turn me off here. I know many can relate to the comment made by former Notre Dame President, Theodore Hesburgh, who once said, "Whenever I feel the need to exercise, I lie down until it passes." For most of us, however, at this time of our lives this attitude can be deadly. Seriously.

For the generation brought up with Jack LaLanne, exercise is a quality of life issue and "this generation expects, indeed demands, to be able to exercise well into their 70's," says Dr. Nicholas A. DiNubile, a Philadelphia area orthopedic surgeon, who coined and trademarked the term boomeritis. Boomeritis is the phenomenon affecting these people who have grown up, encouraged to exercise three to five times a week, and now need the variety of orthopedic surgeries that result.[1]

"Evolution doesn't work that quick. Physically, you can't necessarily do at 50 what you did at 25. We've worn out the warranty on some body parts. That's why so many boomers are breaking down. It ought to be called Generation Ouch," according to Dr. DiNubile. [2]

Health care professionals say baby boomers can extend the warranty on their aging frames. Finding balance in the type of exercise that we continue to do is critical. Dr. DiNubile states that "If people find help getting in balance, there is no reason we all can't keep exercising because it is good for you and it makes you feel good." [3]

Previous thinking was that the human body gradually deteriorated and finally collapsed but now we know that this process can not only be slowed down; it can be reversed. Research has shown that even those in their 90's can still build muscles and increase their aerobic capacity. In fact, the AARP website says that "even people in advanced years (age 90 and older) respond to exercise with a marked and rapid improvement in fitness and function." [4]

"Staying fit," they continue, "will slow the functional decline common with aging, such as loss of muscle strength and weight gain, which makes it difficult to do simple things like shopping and housecleaning. **The overall death rate**

Copyright 2001 by Randy Glasbergen.
www.glasbergen.com

"The handle on your recliner does not qualify as an exercise machine."

is three times higher for those who are sedentary compared to those who are fit." [5]

For those who have exercise already built into their lives, you're a step ahead but for those who don't, please think of anything you can do to consistently (at least three days a week) get you up and your blood circulating. If exercise hasn't had a place in your life, now is the time to reorder or order your priorities.

There are many who haven't had an active life…we've been too busy or we simply don't like it so it has never been a priority. But exercise doesn't have to be grueling. The fact of the matter is this…at this time in your life, anything to do is better than nothing.

Find something, anything, to get you moving. It doesn't even have to be with a goal of losing weight or accomplishing anything noteworthy. The goal is to not allow yourself to become totally sedentary. The goal is to do whatever you need to do to find something that you find enjoyable that involves physical activity. If you don't enjoy it, it will be easy to talk yourself out of it and it will be like most New Year's Resolutions…quickly forgotten.

I've had a history of walking or bike riding which I continued for several years after retiring and moving. I've also discovered that using the pool is perfect exercise and I don't mean "serious" swimming. When it's too hot to walk, walk in the pool. If you normally walk for 30 minutes then walk for 30 minutes in the shallow end of the pool. You'll use muscles you don't normally use and women with hair issues…your hair doesn't get wet AND you don't get hot and sweaty!

I've joined Curves, a fitness experience for women only. There are other similar clubs and similar ones for men. It's 30 minutes of structured, no-brain exercise for a minimum of 3 times per week. I haven't lost a pound but it's only doing good. It would be far more harmful if I did nothing.

Your key to a reFIRED life has to start with good physical and mental health.

Now, what are other priorities in your day? In your life? Give it some thought right now and list some of them below.

1. _____

2. _____

3. _____

4. _____

5. _____

Keys to ReFIREment

Your key to a reFIRED life has to start with good physical and mental health.

Chapter 9

A different kind of busy... but by choice!

After 32 years in Social Services (AKA Welfare Administration), Jill Dinsmore of Redding, California, couldn't wait to retire. She had promised a friend that she would help her run her veterinary clinic, and that was a fulltime job but something she loved. "I never expected to be this busy and I NEVER expected to go back to school." However, while she never had a desire to be a doctor, the administrative hearings that she'd done for years were "kind of law-like," she thought. They realized that adding some law expertise to the practice would be perfect. Jill was more than willing but the closest law school was a commute of 70 miles. Enter the internet...

She found a law school online, which gives her the best of both....no commute, study when she can, no time wasted finding parking or driving, and a challenging curriculum. And, "I am FINALLY able to do what I wanted to do when I grew up...if I ever did!"

Jill says, "My friends are amazed that I would take another job but school just floors them...not only that I signed up for it, but that I am almost through it, with one more year and a bit (4 year program), then the bar. I'm just amazed at how hard I am working to keep up in school."

Jill found that "old brains really aren't tired out, although getting back to school (it had been 30 years since completing her BA) was traumatic, especially the word TEST!"

*Advice from Jill: "**If your job has been your life, you will just curl up and die.** I've seen too many people do that. Take advantage of the time, and have fun. Go learn something new, just to keep your mind stimulated, and so that you will want to get up in the morning so you can get back to what you want to do. Check out new places and new people. Try new experiences...you are not getting any younger! **It's a different kind of busy but by choice.**"*

Take a break. There is no hurry to rush into your new life and the one thing you don't want is to feel pressured to "do something." While decisions you make right now don't have the same kind of permanence that previous decisions in your life might have had, still...enjoy your new freedom. You'll know when it's time to begin adding to your life. You might think you won't ever want to do something else but most people will. Just let your own "gut" tell you when it's time but enjoy your vacation time right now. Vacation time? Yes, vacation time. That's what it is. You've worked for it; you've earned it and it's a great feeling knowing that you don't have to cram everything into this vacation because you don't have to go back to work in a few weeks. In fact, your first few days might really feel like true vacation days. It's after time has gone by and you realize that you're really not going back to work that it finally hits. Lydia Henry of Roseville, California, sums it up this way: "Just remember that retirement is what you earn for all your years of working so enjoy every minute of it." Now, go back to the end of the last chapter. What are your other priorities?

For many this is the time to give back. Retired baby boomers are volunteering at a rate that has risen from 25% in 2002 to 30% in 2004.[1] Volunteering, taking classes, working (even for minimum wage) in an area that you enjoy will keep you reFIRED. There is not a single non-profit organization that can't use volunteers, even if it's only help with mailings. The most important thing for you is that they're generally stress-free. You can finally walk out of there and not take your work problems home with you. They're someone else's problems now.

Most places are desperate for volunteer help and that can be you if you're willing to forget "who you were" and not look at things too menial for you.

That was another life. Get over it! Most organizations will be delighted to have someone who can spell and file and write. Most organizations will be delighted to have a volunteer with a work ethic and a sense of commitment. And, most organizations will provide you with the opportunity to feel that you're doing something very worthwhile.

The phrase "Will work for food" could apply to you if you want to volunteer and if your income is low. It's possible to volunteer at an organization called SHARE. SHARE has branches around the country that distributes food. The acronym stands for Self Help And Resource Exchange. Volunteering for two hours a week makes you eligible for groceries, often at about half the price. To find out more about SHARE, search the internet. Different cities and states have their own website. See if there's one in your area.

Consider any organizations that you believe in. Offer your help to a school in your area or be a mentor. Volunteer at a hospital. Volunteer organizations are limitless. However, be very careful as there is such a thing as volunteer burnout. I would suggest selecting one or two to start with. Again, this has to do with creating balance. It's much easier to add things than it is to get "uninvolved" or cut back if you see you're overextended. It might also be possible that an organization isn't as much fun or as interesting as it appeared. Let's face it...personalities definitely are a factor and your favorite charity might have board members or staff that you don't enjoy working with. Take your time to find out what you really enjoy and what doesn't work for you in the way you thought it might.

This is the important thing to remember...you don't have to continue doing something you're not enjoying! Be mindful of your commitments but here is a perfect example of the freedom to create the life that is balanced, rewarding and pleasant.

Daniel Kadlec points out that one of the distinctions of this group of retirees is that "they are an emerging face of philanthropy. Collectively, regular people who have just retired or are approaching retirement age are making their distinctive mark as social entrepreneurs. Why not?" he asks. "They are part of the healthiest retirement generation to date." And Marc Freedman, founder and president of Civic Ventures, a think tank dedicated to helping people find personally rewarding careers and volunteer work as they age, observes that "A second, non-core career with a focus on service will be their hallmark." [2]

Robert Chambers, 62, had a career in computer services and decided he was ready to cut back so he left that and began selling cars. As time went on he became very disillusioned with the sales tactics that were used, especially on the people least able to be overcharged. "He decided to found a non-profit organization he calls Bonnie CLAC (Car Loans and Counseling), that attempts to negotiate fair car prices for the working poor and offers them low rate loans. Since launching his firm five years ago in New Hampshire, he has underwritten $10 million in loans, and his clients have saved an average of $7,000 over the life of their loan." [3]

I have not done what I said. When I retired and moved I jumped into everything. The good thing was that it provided great opportunities to meet people. The bad thing was that I was so busy that I had little time for myself. I'm a person who needs to be busy so I didn't even mind that…usually. People often said, "I thought you were retired. You're too busy." And my reply always was, "Yes, I'm very busy but it's a choice. I can end it at any time when I no longer enjoy it." And, I have. Knowing, in the back of your mind, that you're not stuck in a situation for years makes all the difference in the world.

And, let me remind you AGAIN of one of the most important keys to a reFIRED life…**you've retired from your job, not from life!**

In addition to volunteering, other possibilities fall under the categories of hobbies, learning something new, getting a job or traveling.

Learning something new can be something complex or simple. I'm actually enrolled at our local community college in the degree program for Graphic Arts. I'm pretty sure I'll never get a degree but taking the courses and becoming minimally knowledgeable in Desktop Publishing, website design and other computer design programs has been challenging but enjoyable. And, who cares if I don't get an A in the class? For once, I can take classes I enjoy and not have anything hanging on how well I do in the course. It's just for me.

Don't be afraid to sign up for degree classes or continuing education classes. I was a little concerned when I started about being an elderly person in a college class. Guess what? There were far more of "us" than there were of "them." Age has never been an issue. If that's holding you back, it won't work. Look at the newest catalogue or go online to the website of your nearest school. Check out the possibilities and then follow Nike's advice...Just Do It!

If you've had hobbies, they're just waiting for you to give them more time and attention. After all, you always said, "when I have the time," didn't you? If you haven't seriously had a hobby but you have an interest, this is the time to turn that interest into something more. Time and money are the two things that often prevent people from developing hobbies further. The time is now. Everyone's financial situation is different and an individual challenge but priorities help you with your own situation.

Have you always thought you'd like to write? For many of us, that involved a book, poetry, articles. Fortunately for us, a new opportunity for writing has come along and they're called Blogs…short for web logs. If you're computer savvy at all, starting your own blog is very easy and can be on any subject you're interested in. One of the sites where you can easily create your own blog is at www.blogster.com and statistics from that site indicate that 22% of its bloggers are older than 50, a 20% increase in one year!

Every Saturday morning for years I have received a "missive" from Joe Klock. Joe says he is 80 and "somewhat over his fighting weight." In his previous life, he excelled in sales, management, training, lecturing and counseling. He cautions me that he retired TO "wordsmithery." Besides his weekly opinion columns, which have appeared in over 200 publications nationwide, he has a book, a website (www. joeklock.com), audio products and ezines on Sales Tips and Management Tips. His book, "Like Klockwork…the Whimsy, Wit and (sometime) Wisdom of a Key Largo Curmudgeon" is a collection of 88 of his short essays. While you may not always agree with his pieces, they are usually witty and funny. His own self-assessment is that "he is long-winded on the platform, short-winded on the stairs, has absolutely no wholesome hobbies and is instinctively disliked by small dogs. Also, he drinks, swears, bites his fingernails, and entertains impure thoughts…often simultaneously." He also says that he is "afflicted with distinguished creditors, disreputable friends, highly influential enemies, a variety of post-menopausal ailments, athlete's foot and a hernia. (From some of these maladies, he has recovered.)" Wordsmithery…a perfect word and a perfect "hobby" for Joe Klock. While he does do some freelance writing, most of it is simply for enjoyment. But his enjoyment provides the same for many.

Another activity is to get a job. Get a job? I just got out of a job! The U.S. Bureau of Labor Statistics reports that when workers over age 45 were asked about their work plans during retirement, 69% said they plan to work in some capacity during retirement. Only 28% said they were not planning to work at all.

I wouldn't get a job for awhile. You deserve this break and you'll know when it's time to start thinking about it. Even though you probably thought you wouldn't get a job after retiring, many people eventually do...in situations they never dreamed of doing.

For those of us who are not independently wealthy, it doesn't take long to realize that your pension and social security provide you with pretty basic needs. I appreciate that but a little supplemental income, generated from an enjoyable job, helps.

Hopefully you can find a part-time job that is satisfying and gets you out of your house. Dr. Roger Gillis, a retired dentist from Illinois, and his wife, Kathleen, moved to a new location. She opened her own business but Roger is job sharing with another person at his local newspaper, taking classified ads. It's perfect for both and...they both love it! I'm sure neither of these professionals ever anticipated, in their previous lives, that they would ever be doing something like they're doing now. But, that was then; this is now. It's perfect. The newspaper has two intelligent people taking ads and these two former professionals are keeping busy a couple of days a week in an enjoyable setting. And, just remember...if they don't like it, they don't have to stay. Dr. Gillis says, "I was always in the people business and I'm back in a job with a lot of interaction with people. Forget about what you used to be! Figure out what's fun, doesn't take all your time and provides you flexibility. For me, this is perfect!"

Another job option is a new idea with great possibilities. Time Magazine's Lisa Takeuchi Cullen refers to this new stage as the "not-quite retirement." Cullen says that "as life spans lengthen, pensions tighten and workplace rules change, hopping from full-time work to full-time leisure is appearing less realistic and, to some, less desirable. The

Retired dentist, Dr. Roger Gillis, at his job
taking classified ads at a newspaper.

trend has given rise to a new category of employment, the so-called *bridge job*. Economists use the term to describe part-time or full-time jobs typically held for less than 10 years following full-time careers." [4]

A bridge job seems to be a win-win for the 'retiree' and the company. Cullen points out that as the 76 million baby boomers begin to retire, economists project a labor shortage. Hiring these people using a "bridge" model provides companies with loyalty, productivity and an undervalued commodity: wisdom.

Finally, travel. Travel is one of those things that many put off for varying reasons. I've traveled some but there's a lot more I'd like to do. However, now that I have the time, I really don't have the money.

Here are a couple of suggestions if money is an issue.

Elderhostel is a great group to travel with if you don't demand luxury accommodations. It is moderately priced but the important thing that makes Elderhostel unique is that participants go to learn. All of the destinations have programs where people learn in depth about a location from local experts. I've spoken to the Elderhostel groups that come to Key West and I've been very impressed with the organization and the quality of the travelers in the group.

Another possibility for cruising is to be a presenter on a cruise. Ships always have destination speakers, special interest speakers, bridge tournament organizers, dance instructors, computer teachers and other entertainers. Entertainers are paid but the others are not. They are, however, given very reduced rates so that opportunities for inexpensive traveling abound if you feel comfortable sharing information. This is where your hobby might come in to play. They are always looking for "how to" presentations. These days, "scrapbooking" is a special interest. If your hobby is bridge, you and your spouse could take a working cruise, coordinating bridge competitions. One friend has degrees in art and in history. She and her husband have traveled around the world, scheduling 6 working cruises per year, with her speaking about the art and history of the countries that they are cruising to. And, did I tell you…you can bring another person? I recently returned from a 10-day cruise to the Mexican Riviera and look forward to future, inexpensive, working cruises. The company I use is Sixth Star Entertainment. Look online at www.sixthstar.com. This is a perfect way to put your hobbies, your talents or your special interests to work for you and help you to travel inexpensively.

Does this help with ideas? If not, think, research and then, take action.

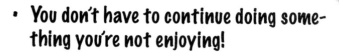

Keys to ReFIREment

- **You don't have to continue doing something you're not enjoying!**
- **Forget what you used to be. That was then; this is now!**

Chapter 10

Building your life résumé.

Robert Lopatin spent his pre Life, Part II, days running a women's clothing company for 27 years with his father. They sold the business in 1990 and Lopatin decided that it wasn't too late to fulfill his boyhood dream of becoming a doctor. As one of the oldest first year residents in the country at age 55, he said, "It's like nirvana. I feel like I died and was born again."

Dr. Lopatin asks, "How many times is a person genuinely free to be able to restart their life?"

*"I said to myself, 'I have to at least pursue it because if I don't **I will be forever filled with self-reproach. I will have failed myself**."*

Lopatin's prescription (and another key) for a fulfilling, no-regrets life: Don't be afraid of change and never pass up an opportunity to try something new.[1]

Probably starting in high school we began to hear of the future importance of a résumé. The classes we selected, the organizations we participated in, the leadership roles we attained, our talents, and our hobbies...all began to be the basis of a résumé that would help us. From that time forward, whether you realized it or not, your life was taking the form of a résumé. In most cases, the purpose of that résumé was for job applications.

Now we're to a point where that résumé might not be as vital as it once was. (I'm still amused, when I fill out an app for one of my little part time jobs, when I have to list my elementary school. A lot of water has flowed under the bridge since then!) Nevertheless it is in some ways the most fun and most interesting when you look at how you want that life résumé to look when it's finished.

Now's the time. What are those things you always wanted to do? What are those skills that you always wanted to learn? Where are those places that you always wanted to visit? What are those jobs that you never had an opportunity to do? Where is that place you always wanted to live? What is that goal you always wanted to accomplish?

The best thing about creating your life résumé is that it doesn't have to make sense to anyone but you. This is assuming that your significant relationships value your desire to make the best of Life, Part II. And, this is assuming that only you can make choices and decisions based on circumstances

"I'm writing about all the things I ought to do before I die. It's my oughtobiography."

specifically yours. But, building your life résumé is about attitude more than anything else. It's the glass half full attitude; it's the can-do attitude; it's the "reFIRED" attitude.

We have talked about it earlier. Start with the end in mind. When it's all said and done, what do you want that résumé to say? Your life will be neatly packaged in that summary.

If you don't know how to start, think about a résumé. What are the categories that are usually asked for? Some things don't lend themselves to change but most do.

We've talked about taking classes. If you do that, add any class under the category of education.

"Jack Rothman, a former professor of public affairs at UCLA devotes himself to a favorite activity in his senior years. But Rothman's is not one of the customary retirement pastimes – not golf or travel or genealogy or a reading club. No, Rothman's pursuit is a lot more laughs than those, but it's also more difficult and, to some, much scarier. It's stand-up comedy.

Rothman's performing instincts blossomed when his three children gave him a gift certificate for stand-up comedy classes on his 75th birthday." [2]

According to Time Magazine's Laura Koss-Feder, "managers, club owners and comedy instructors estimate that the phenomenon of seniors taking the plunge into stand up comedy has grown 25%-50% in the last five years!"

"What's behind it? A turbulent world that needs some making fun of, the inspiration of new comic venues, the increased time seniors have in their lives to explore passions and hobbies, and a sense of not caring what others think and of doing their own thing that characterizes the baby-boomer mindset." [3]

That attitude was reflected by Sally Field when asked if she was interested in 'meeting' someone and getting involved again. Field replied, "When you're old, you are more certain of who you are, and that may be a good thing or a bad thing." She adds, "Because you've lived your life, you're independent, you're not looking for anyone to 'complete you', as the saying is. There isn't anyone who would complete me. I am so *way* completed." [4] In other words, you might have cared earlier in life if you didn't have a significant other. Now, what others think…about anything… is not your problem.

You don't have to be a part of something as mind blowing as the group formed in Northampton, Massachusetts, called the Young@Heart Chorus. The group is made up of 70, 80 and 90-year-olds that perform rock and roll classics. What's more…they tour around the world. Without a doubt, they are extraordinary. One of the members, Brock Lynch, 80, describes the group as "hip, hot and hams!" [5] Check out their website at www.youngatheartchorus.com.

Another group that has made its mark is the Fabulous Palm Springs Follies, a group comprised of performers who range in age from 55-80+. When they were formed, people scoffed and said "Who's going to pay to see old ladies' legs?" How wrong they were! To be inspired by a group of "mature" women, go to www.psfollies.com.

Résumés have a section about employment. While thinking of your life résumé, do you want to add any more employment experiences? Maybe there's no choice but maybe there is… you just want something to do on occasion. You might end up being a greeter at Wal-Mart even though you were a stock broker in your previous life. Add it. It's all ultimately part of the quilt that is being created with every experience you have. Do you want that quilt to be made of gray sweatshirt material or do you want it to be colorful bits and pieces of your life…big, small, odd shaped…that form the finished product.

You are the one with lots of time now to concentrate on perhaps the biggest and most important goal of your life. Your life is only partially shaped.

As trite as it may sound, THE FUTURE IS NOW. Don't let it pass you by without your active participation. This is your job now. Do it for you. Do it now. Do it right!

Keys to ReFIREment

- The best thing about creating your life résumé is that it doesn't have to make sense to anyone but you.

Chapter 11

Die with your boots on...
red or not!

Amy Weishaus *taught English and Journalism for 33 years in Pearl River, NY, but when she retired, she moved to Florida (it's the law!) and took advantage of her dream of becoming an entrepreneur.... finally. She had the opportunity to do anything, but a gift basket of books that she made for a hospitalized friend in 1991 made her realize that she had stumbled onto something promising.*

Her son suggested she call her business Basket o' Books (www.basketobooks.com) and her personalized creations include books, CD's, DVD's and gourmet items. She services both corporate and personal accounts.

Amy feels that this venture is a perfect fit which matches her previous English/Journalism career with a desire to own her own business. "Teaching," she says, "was about books, people and stories; the baskets are a very natural and comfortable transition. They're about caring and compassion." Surely someone who worked with young people for 33 years displays these traits as part of her innate fiber. In her case, she works out of her home because retirement affords more flexibility and less structure.

Moving to a new location means making new friends and in a business like hers, the best advertising is word of mouth referrals. Amy has joined NPI (Network Professionals Incorporated) and the local Chamber of Commerce. Networking is vital for the

*success of her business, and these organizations
have "opened lots of new doors. As a result, I've
made wonderful friends as well."*

*Amy's advice: "Don't lose the passion. Keep doing!
Keep open to endless possibilities!"*

When you hear the expression that someone "died with
their boots on," what does that mean to you? It's a
more colorful expression than "don't slow down until you
cross the finish line." But, don't they both mean the same
thing? Amy just said it: **"Keep doing."**

Let me be the contrarian to the thoughts and attitudes
of many people whose mentality is that retiring...the end
of Life, Part I, is the beginning of the end. There's no way
to dispute that but as I've pointed out, Life, Part II, has the
potential to be THE MOST EXCITING, REWARDING,
ENJOYABLE part of the entire production. That doesn't
happen accidentally. It happens because you're in a reFIRED
frame of mind. You're not sitting in your recliner, staring out
the window, wondering how you're going to fill your time.
You might be sitting in your recliner planning how you're
going to fit it all in.

Unlike many goals or plans, this one has an undefined
ending. That means there's no time to waste. That means it's
not time to slow down in the example of the finish line. Of
course, you're going to slow down when you refer to your
pre-retirement years. My point is this...your new life involves a new way of participating in it. Because you have

more choices and options, fewer obligations and a reFIRED attitude, you can embrace this phase with zeal and optimism.

When I was in high school, I loved to square dance and a little group of ours won the Indiana Square Dancing contest one year. I loved any kind of dancing and taught it in later years. I don't mind telling you that I was GOOD! However, my husband didn't like to dance so when I got married, I never did any dancing of any kind. When I retired and moved to Key West I read that there was a line dancing class held weekly about 30 miles away and I decided that line dancing was something that I could easily get back in to. It had been years (and about 100 pounds ago) but I knew I would pick it up quickly and I would be so happy to be dancing again.

The truth of the matter is…I wasn't good and I didn't pick it up quickly like I used to. I was a real amateur yet I had minored in Dance Education in college. What a shock! What a realization to come to grips with. After many weeks of driving up there and not getting any better, I finally threw in the towel. When I told a friend about my lack of success, she said, "You know I'm confidant that if you'd just had the red boots you would have been great!" That made me feel better. I now had a great excuse…I would have been good if I'd just had the red boots.

What are your "red boots?" What excuses do you use? They're common and people use them all the time:

- How do I even know where to begin?
- Are you kidding? I could never do that!
- I don't know anyone
- Who would I do it with?

When Jill Dinsmore was having her pre-acceptance interview for law school, she must have been looking for some excuse to bail her out of her crazy idea of starting law school. She told the interviewer, "I'll be 59 when I graduate." He cut her no slack. His response, probably one that changed her life at that moment, was, "Yeah, and you'll be 59 if you don't!" Whatever your red boots ex-

Author, (2nd from left) and Columbus, (Indiana)
High School square dancing friends – **1959**.

cuse is, don't let it get in the way of achieving something meaningful, as I did.

Time Magazine's Nancy Gibbs, in an article called "Midlife Crisis? Bring It On!" describes how "women are seizing that stressful, pivotal moment in their lives to reinvent themselves." [1] While her points are specifically about women and a midlife crisis, I see the parallels with sorting out how we are going to live a reFIRED life,

She says that women are "confronting the obstacles of middle age and figuring out how to turn them into opportunities. Thanks to higher incomes, better education and long experience at juggling multiple roles, women may actually discover that there has never been a better time to have a midlife crisis than now."[1] I suggest that this is exactly what I have been saying about being fortunate enough to retire now. Opportunities are endless…for everyone…not just women!

What does it take? It takes the courage to try. Often what happens in the trying is more important than the end result. Trying often results in failure but trying is the key. I tried to line dance. I never was able to recapture my great dancing skill but the trying made it fun.

"The process is more important than the prize," explains Grady Jim Robinson, a master storyteller. Grady Jim uses the example of Michael Johnson, a 200-yard Olympic sprinter. "He likes the beginning of the race more than the end." Why? The adventure is about to happen…it's the process…at the end, he wins and it's great but he says it's the thrill of doing it. Men look for the prize; women know that the process is far more important." [2]

You're continuing this run for your life and you're doing it without removing those boots. Don't take them off and don't slow down. Look at the prize but enjoy the journey. **Keep doing!**

Keys to ReFIREment

- **Your new life involves a new way of participating in it.**
- **It takes the courage to try**
- **Don't slow down; enjoy the journey!**

Chapter 12

"Woo Hoo, what a ride!"

> *Life should NOT be a journey to the grave with the intention of arriving safely in an attractive and well preserved body, but rather to skid in sideways, chocolate in one hand, wine in the other, body thoroughly used up, totally worn out and screaming, "Woo Hoo, what a ride!"*

I get such enjoyment out of this quotation. You've probably seen it, too. I don't know who the author is but if you know, please let me know so I can give credit where credit is due. It's had such an impact on me because the visual it provides is priceless.

The message talks about NOT arriving safely but arriving safely might be exactly YOU. You might prefer the status quo. You might be "buttoned down." You might not like taking risks. But, you might be that way and not like it. You might be in that proverbial "rut." Why? Is it because you've always been that way? Is it because of looking foolish? Is it because someone might disapprove?

There is a limit to the time we have. If you like the concept of arriving "safely," by all means, do it and enjoy.

But, if you're in a rut and see the opportunity for change, taking risks and reinventing, I hope I've given you plenty of suggestions and ideas.

What I'm really saying is, "Folks, do it your way." We were the ones who grew up with Frank Sinatra singing "My

Way." Now we can. "My way" might not be "your way" but it's what works for you. There is no right or wrong. The important thing is to make sure that whatever you're doing is on purpose. Most of all, *MINIMIZE REGRETS!*

Taking advantage of Life, Part II, and filling it with a "reFIRED" life gives us the perfect opportunity to take that slide and make this quote our own.

Keys to ReFIREment

- Minimize regrets
- Never lose your sense of humor

But wait, there's more...it ain't over 'til the fat lady sings and I'm just getting warmed up....

Chapter 13

Save the last laugh for ME!

You know you're old when...

- they retire your blood type (Phyllis Diller)
- going braless stretches the wrinkles out of your face
- you go for a mammogram and realize it's the only time someone's going to ask you to go topless
- you refer to your waterbed as the dead sea
- you're sitting in your rocker and can't get it started
- you're asleep but others think you're dead
- you hear snap, crackle and pop at the breakfast table and you're not eating cereal
- you try to straighten out the wrinkles in your socks and discover you're not wearing any
- you and your teeth don't sleep together
- a young babe catches your fancy and your pacemaker opens your garage door
- your idea of weightlifting is standing up
- an 'all nighter' means not getting up to go to the bathroom
- the only two things we do with greater frequency in middle age are urinate and attend funerals
- it takes two tries to get up from the couch
- it takes longer to rest than it did to get tired
- the only whistles you get are from the tea kettle
- you get winded playing chess
- the little old lady you helped cross the street is your wife

- your children look middle-aged
- your knees buckle and your belt won't
- you bite into an apple and your teeth stay there
- your back goes out more than you do
- you are proud of your lawn mower
- your best friend is dating someone half his age... and isn't breaking any laws
- you sing along with the elevator music
- you have a dream about prunes
- your ears are hairier than your head
- "getting lucky" means finding your car in the parking lot
- the end of your tie doesn't come anywhere near the top of your pants (what tie?)
- you can live without sex but not without glasses
- you go into the next room to get something and can't remember what you came for
- you look into the mirror and are shocked to see that "old person" looking back at you
- a 30-year mortgage sounds like a pretty clever scam
- you look at your know-it-all, beeper-wearing teen-ager and think, "For this I have stretch marks?"
- the gleam in your eyes is from the sun hitting your bifocals
- your secrets are safe with your friends because they can't remember them either

- you want to grab every firm young lovely in a tube top and scream, "Listen, honey, even the Roman Empire fell and those will, too!"

- the growth of hair on our legs slows down allowing us time to concentrate on the growth of our new mustache

- you find greener pastures but you can't climb the fence

- you stop to think…and forget to start again

- you fall down and wonder what else you can do while you're down there

- what doesn't hurt, doesn't work

- a dripping tap causes an uncontrollable urge

- when happy hour is a nap

- you stand naked in front of a mirror and see your rear without turning around

- women no longer have upper arms but instead of wingspans

- you tend to repeat yourself

- you tend to repeat yourself'

- you tend to repeat yourself!
  (STOP…you sound like a broken record.
  Try saying that to a kid today!)

How to Stay Young

1. Try everything twice. On Madams tombstone (of Whelan's and Madam…whoever/whatever that is) she said she wanted this epitaph: Tried everything twice…loved it both times!
2. Keep only cheerful friends. The grouches pull you down. (Keep this in mind if you are one of those grouches.)
3. Keep learning: Learn more about the computer, crafts, gardening, whatever. Never let the brain get idle. "An idle mind is the devil's workshop." And the devil's name is Alzheimer's!
4. Enjoy the simple things.
5. Laugh often, long and loud. Laugh until you gasp for breath. And if you have a friend who makes you laugh, spend lots and lots of time with HIM/HER.
6. The tears happen: Endure, grieve, and move on. The only person who is with us our entire life, is ourselves. LIVE while you are alive.
7. Surround yourself with what you love: Whether it's family, pets, keepsakes, music, plants, hobbies, whatever Your home is your refuge.
8. Cherish your health: If it is good, preserve it. If it is unstable, improve it. If it is beyond what you can improve, get help.
9. Don't take guilt trips. Take a trip to the mall, even to the next county, to a foreign country, but NOT to where the guilt is.
10. Tell the people you love that you love them, at every opportunity.
11. Forgive now those who made you cry. You might not get a second time.

Jokes and Quotations for Women

An elderly woman died last month. Having never married, she requested no male pallbearers. In her handwritten instructions for her memorial service, she wrote, "They wouldn't take me out while I was alive, I don't want them to take me out when I'm dead."

* * * * *

Maya Angelou was interviewed by Oprah on her 70+ birthday. Oprah asked her what she thought of growing older. And, there on television, she said it was "exciting." Regarding body changes, she said "there were many, occurring every day...like her breasts. They seem to be in a race to see which will reach her waist, first."

* * * * *

"After a certain age, if you don't wake up aching somewhere, you may be dead."   – Maxine

* * * * *

"I do my housework in the nude. It gives me an incentive to clean the mirrors as quickly as possible." – Maxine

* * * * *

"This is so amazing. I am 53 years old but I feel like I'm 16. And if I wasn't in the middle of a hot flash, I'd believe that!"   – S. Epatha Merkerson

* * * * *

"I'm just a 16 year old girl locked in an old ladies body."
— Unknown

* * * * *

"I'm going south for the winter...actually some of my parts are headed there already."   — Maxine

* * * * *

"The years that a woman subtracts from her age are not lost. They're added on to other women's."
— Diane dePoiters

* * * * *

I'm out of estrogen and I have a gun.
— Too many to mention

* * * * *

In the not too distant past
I remember very well
Grandmas tended to their knitting,
and their cookies were just swell.
They were always at the ready,
when you needed some advice.
And their sewing (I can tell you)
was available .. and nice.

Well, Grandma's not deserted you,
she dearly loves you still
You just won't find her cooking,
but she's right there at the till.

She thinks about you daily
you haven't been forsook.
Your photos are quite handy,
in the Pentium notebook.
She scans your art work now though,
and combines it with cool sounds,
to make electronic greetings.
She prints pictures by the pound.

She's right there when you need her,
you really aren't alone,
She's out now with her "'puter pals,"
but she took her new cell phone.
You can also leave a message
on her answering machine;
or page her at the fun meet;
She's been there since eight fifteen.

Yes, the world's a very different place,
there is no doubt of that.
So "E" her from her web page,
or join her in a chat.
She's joined the electronic age,
and it really seems to suit her.

So don't expect the same old gal,
cause Grandma's gone "Computer"

Jokes and Quotations for Men

"By the time a man is wise enough to watch his step, he's too old to go anywhere."
— Billy Crystal

* * * * *

"A man is not old until regrets take the place of dreams."
— John Barrymore

* * * * *

An elderly man in Florida had owned a large farm for several years. He had a large pond in the back, fixed up nice; picnic tables, horseshoe courts, and some apple and peach trees. The pond was properly shaped and fixed up for swimming when it was built. One evening the old farmer decided to go down to the pond, as he hadn't been there for a while, and look it over. He grabbed a five gallon bucket to bring back some fruit.

As he neared the pond, he heard voices shouting and laughing with glee. As he came closer he saw it was a bunch of young women skinny-dipping in his pond. He made the women aware of his presence and they all went to the deep end. One of the women shouted to him, "We're not coming out until you leave!"

The old man frowned, "I didn't come down here to watch you ladies swim naked or make you get out of the pond naked." Holding the bucket up he said, "I'm here to feed the alligator."

Moral: Old men can still think fast.

* * * * *

A very elderly gentleman, (mid nineties) very well dressed, hair well groomed, great looking suit, flower in his lapel, smelling slightly of a good after shave, presenting a well looked-after image, walks into an upscale cocktail lounge. Seated at the bar is an elderly looking lady, in her mid-eighties.

The gentleman walks over, sits alongside of her, orders a drink, takes a sip, turns to her and says, "So tell me, do I come here often?"

* * * * *

A man was telling his neighbor, "I just bought a new hearing aid. It cost me four thousand dollars, but it's state of the art. It's perfect." "Really," answered the neighbor. "What kind is it?" "Twelve thirty."

* * * * *

Morris, an 82 year-old man, went to the doctor to get a physical. A few days later, the doctor saw Morris walking down the street with a gorgeous young woman on his arm.

A couple of days later, the doctor spoke to Morris and said, "You're really doing great, aren't you?"

Morris replied, "Just doing what you said, Doc: 'Get a hot mamma and be cheerful.'"

The doctor said, "I didn't say that. I said, 'You've got a heart murmur; be careful.'"

* * * * *

An elderly gentleman had serious hearing problems for a number of years. He went to the doctor and the doctor was able to have him fitted for a set of hearing aids that allowed the gentleman to hear 100%.

The elderly gentleman went back in a month to the doctor and the doctor said, "Your hearing is perfect. Your family must be really pleased that you can hear again."

The gentleman replied, "Oh, I haven't told my family yet. I just sit around and listen to the conversations. I've changed my will three times!"

* * * * *

Two elderly gentlemen from a retirement center were sitting on a bench under a tree when one turns to the other and says: "Slim, I'm 83 years old now and I'm just full of aches and pains. I know you're about my age. How do you feel?"

Slim says, "I feel just like a newborn baby."

"Really!? Like a newborn baby!?"

"Yep. No hair, no teeth, and I think I just wet my pants.

* * * * *

A senior citizen said to his eighty-year old buddy: "So I hear you're getting married?"

"Yep!"

"Do I know her?"

"Nope!"

"This woman, is she good looking?"

"Not really."

"Is she a good cook?"

"N aw, she can't cook too well."

"Does she have lots of money?"

"Nope! Poor as a church mouse."

"Well, then, is she good in bed?"

"I don't know."

"Why in the world do you want to marry her then?"

"Because she can still drive!"

*   *   *   *   *

Hospital regulations require a wheelchair for patients being discharged. However, while working as a student nurse, I found one elderly gentleman – already dressed and sitting on the bed with a suitcase at his feet –who insisted he didn't need my help to leave the hospital.

After a chat about rules being rules, he reluctantly let me wheel him to the elevator. On the way down I asked him if his wife was meeting him.

"I don't know," he said. "She's still upstairs in the bathroom changing out of her hospital gown."

Middle Age and Getting Old

"Getting old is a walk in the park...where no one picks up after their dog."   – Maxine

* * * * *

"Aging seems to be the only available way to live a long life."   – Daniel Abner

* * * * *

"Middle age is when your age starts to show around your middle."   – Bob Hope

* * * * *

"To keep the heart unwrinkled, to be hopeful, kindly, cheerful, reverent—that is to triumph over old age."
–Thomas Bailey Aldrich

* * * * *

"While we have the gift of life, it seems to me the only tragedy is to allow part of us to die...whether it is our spirit, our creativity or our glorious uniqueness."   –Gilda Radner

* * * * *

"Don't worry about avoiding temptation. As you grown older, it will avoid you."   – Winston Churchill

* * * * *

"Gray hair is God's graffiti."   – Bill Cosby

* * * * *

"We could certainly slow down the aging process if it had to work its way through Congress."   – Will Rogers

* * * * *

"I don't feel old. I don't feel anything until noon. Then I take a nap."   – Bob Hope

* * * * *

Life is not measured by the number of breaths we take but by the moments that take our breath away.

* * * * *

"When I was a kid looking at people who were 60, I said, 'Man, there goes an ancient person."

– President George Bush on his 60th Birthday

* * * * *

You're not old; you're chronologically gifted.

* * * * *

"Maybe it's true that life begins at fifty...but everything else starts to wear out, fall out, or spread out."

– Phyllis Diller

* * * * *

The secret to staying young is finding an age you really like and stick with it.

* * * * *

When I was a kid I could toast marshmallows over my birthday candles; now I can roast a turkey!

* * * * *

"To me, old age is always 15 years older than I am."

– Bernard Baruch

* * * * *

"You're never too old to become younger" – Mae West

* * * * *

"Old age is not so bad when you consider the alternatives."   – Maurice Chevalier

* * * * *

Inside every older person is a young person wondering what happened.

* * * * *

It takes about 10 years to get used to how old you are.

* * * * *

Count your life by smiles, not tears.
Count your age by friends, not years.

* * * * *

Don't let an old person crawl inside your body.

* * * * *

There is more money being spent on breast implants and Viagra today than on Alzheimer's research. This means that by 2040, there should be a large elderly population with perky boobs and huge erections and absolutely no recollection of what to do with them.

* * * * *

"The only constant in my life during these retirement years is going to be change."   – Pat Donovan, AZ

* * * * *

Few people know how to be old.

* * * * *

"I just celebrate waking up on the right side of the grass every morning."   – TV Anchor, Linda Ellerbee

* * * * *

"How ironic. Retirement, it seems, is the fountain of youth."   – Elizabeth Pope

* * * * *

I have a photographic memory. Unfortunately it no longer offers same day service.

* * * * *

The woman who tells her age is either too young to have anything to lose or too old to have anything to gain.
                    – Chinese Proverb

* * * * *

"Senior citizens. People say they don't know how to drive. You think it's so easy to maneuver a car on the sidewalk?"
                    – Jack Rothman, 98, LA Comedian

* * * * *

I'm entering the 'metallic' years: silver in my hair, gold in my teeth and lead in my bottom!

* * * * *

Old age comes at a bad time.

* * * * *

Once you're over the hill, you pick up speed.

* * * * *

Life is like a roll of toilet paper...the closer it gets to the end, the faster it goes.

* * * * *

Some people, no matter how old they get, never lose their beauty; they merely move it from their face to their heart.

* * * * *

The older I get, the better I used to be.

* * * * *

Just because you have pains doesn't mean you have to be one!

* * * * *

We do not stop laughing because we grow old; we grow old because we stop laughing.

* * * * *

I'm not old; I'm just a victim of gravity.

* * * * *

I can't figure out if life is passing me by or trying to run me over.

* * * * *

So, these are the golden years. I'm not impressed!

* * * * *

"If you don't stop and look around once in awhile, you'll miss it."   – Ferris Buehler's Day Off

* * * * *

"Take every birthday with a grain of salt. This works much better if the salt accompanies a Margarita." – Maxine

* * * * *

"You never grow old until you've lost all your marvels!"
– Merry Browne

* * * * *

"Don't let aging get you down; it's too hard to get back up."   – Maxine

Just Plain Funny Jokes

I recently picked a new primary care physician. After two visits and exhaustive lab tests, he said I was doing "fairly well for my age."

A little concerned about that comment, I couldn't resist asking him, "Do you think I'll live to be 80?"

He asked, "Well, do you smoke tobacco or drink beer/wine?" "Oh no," I replied. "I'm not doing either."

Then he asked, "Do you eat rib-eye steaks and barbecued ribs?" I said, "No, my other doctor said that all red meat is very unhealthy!"

"Do you spend a lot of time in the sun, like playing golf, sailing, hiking, or bicycling?" No, I don't," I said.

He asked, "Do you gamble, drive fast cars, or have a lot of sex?" "No," I said. "I don't do any of those things."

He looked at me and said, "Then why do you give a care if you live to be 80?"

* * * * *

An elderly Floridian called 911 on her cell phone to report that her car had been broken into. She was hysterical as she explained her situation to the dispatcher: "They've stolen the stereo, the steering wheel, the brake pedal and even the accelerator!" she cried. The dispatcher said, "Stay calm. An officer is on the way." A few minutes later, the officer radios in. "Disregard." He says. "She got in the back-seat by mistake."

* * * * *

Three sisters ages 92, 94 and 96 live in a house together. One night the 96 year old draws a bath. She puts her foot in and pauses. She yells to the other sisters, "Was I getting in or out of the bath?" The 94 year old yells back, "I don't know. I'll come up and see." She starts up the stairs and pauses "Was I going up the stairs or down?" The 92 year old is sitting at the kitchen table having tea listening to her sisters. She shakes her head and says, "I sure hope I never get that forgetful, knock on wood." She then yells, "I'll come up and help both of you as soon as I see who's at the door."

* * * * *

Three retirees, each with a hearing loss, were playing golf one fine March day. One remarked to the other, "Windy, isn't it?" "No," the second man replied, "it's Thursday." And the third man chimed in, "So am I. Let's have a beer."

* * * * *

A little old lady was running up and down the halls in a nursing home. As she walked, she would flip up the hem of her nightgown and say "Supersex." She walked up to an elderly man in a wheelchair. Flipping her gown at him, she said, "Supersex." He sat silently for a moment or two and finally answered, "I'll take the soup."

* * * * *

Two elderly ladies had been friends for many decades. Over the years, they had shared all kinds of activities and adventures. Lately, their activities had been limited to meeting a few times a week to play cards. One day, they were playing cards when one looked at the other and said, "Now don't get mad at me. I know we've been friends for a long time...but I just can't think of your name! I've thought and thought, but I can't remember it. Please tell me what your name is." Her friend glared at her. For at least three minutes she just stared and glared at her. Finally she said, "How soon do you need to know?"

* * * * *

As a senior citizen was driving down the freeway, his car phone rang. Answering, he heard his wife's voice urgently warning him, "Herman, I just heard on the news that there's a car going the wrong way on Interstate 77. Please be careful!" "Heck," said Herman, "It's not just one car. It's hundreds of them!"

* * * * *

Two elderly women were out driving in a large car; both could barely see over the dashboard. As they were cruising along, they came to an intersection. The stoplight was red, but they just went on through. The woman in the passenger seat thought to herself "I must be losing it. I could have sworn we just went through a red light." After a few more minutes, they came to another intersection and the light was red again. Again, they went right through. The woman in the passenger seat was almost sure that the light had been red but was really concerned that she was losing it. She was getting nervous. At the next intersection, sure enough, the light was red and they went on through. So, she turned to the other woman and said, "Mildred, did you know that we just ran through three red lights in a row? You sure could have killed us both!" Mildred turned to her and said, "Oh, crap, am I driving?"

* * * * *

A couple in their nineties, are both having problems remembering things. During a checkup, the doctor tells them that they're physically okay, but they might want to start writing things down to help them remember.

Later that night, while watching TV, the old man gets up from his chair. "Want anything while I'm in the kitchen?" he asks. "Will you get me a bowl of ice cream?" "Sure." "Don't you think you should write it down so you can remember it?" she asks. "No, I can remember it." "Well, I'd like some strawberries on top, too. Maybe you should write it down, so's not to forget it?" He says, "I can remember that. You want a bowl of ice cream with strawberries." "I'd also like whipped cream. I'm certain you'll forget that, write it down?" she asks. Irritated, he says, "I don't need to write it down, I can remember it! Ice cream with strawberries and whipped cream – I got it, for goodness sake! Then he toddles into the kitchen.

After about 20 minutes, the old man returns from the kitchen and hands his wife a plate of bacon and eggs. She stares at the plate for a moment. "Where's my toast?"

Age is...

- a matter of mind over matter and if you don't mind, it don't matter!
- a number; old is in your head.
- a number and mine is unlisted.
- a very high price to pay for maturity.
- like fine wine and cheese...they get better with age.

OK...I hope you enjoyed our time together. Let me say it one more time:

"You've retired from your job; not from life!"

Let me know about your reFIRED life...

and now, use your imagination,

I'M SINGING!

Things I Read and Listened To (Bibliography, in other books)

Chapter 1:
1 Trafford, Abigail, "My Time: Making the Most of the Rest of Your Life."

Chapter 2:
1 Adams, Jane, AARP Bulletin, May, 2006, p.35.
2 Gibbs, Bonnie, "She wasn't ready – now she's making up for lost time," Good Housekeeping, August, 2006, p. 68.

Chapter 3:
1 Pope, Elizabeth, "Tricky Transition," Time Magazine, September, 2005, Bonus Section.

Chapter 4:
1 Edgerton, William, Indiana Alumni Magazine, May/June 1999, p.5.

Chapter 5:
1 Perls, Dr. Thomas, "Your Longevity IQ," AARP Magazine, Sept./Oct, 2006, p. 93.
2 Kadlec, Daniel "New Tricks for Living Past 96," Time Magazine, August 21, 2006.
3 http://www.eons.com
4 Ibid.
5 Parachin, Victor, "It's Never Too Late to Start an Adventure," The Toastmaster, July, 2003, pp.24-25.

Chapter 6:
1 Block, Sandra, USA Today, Partners might want to synchronize goals before retirement closes in," July 25, 2006.
2 Ibid.

3 Mahoney, Sarah, "10 Secrets of a Good, Long Life," AARP, July, 2005.
4 Block
5 Mahoney

Chapter 7:
1 Parachin, Victor, "It's Never Too Late to Start an Adventure," The Toastmaster, July, 2003, pp.24-25.

Chapter 8:
1 Pennington, Bill, New York Times, April 16, 2006, "Baby Boomers Stay Active, and So Do Their Doctors".
2 Ibid.
3 Ibid.
4 AARP Website, "Weight Gain"
5 Ibid.

Chapter 9:
1 US Bureau of Labor Statistics
2 Kadlec, Daniel, "A Car Salesman You Can Trust," Time Magazine, July 31, 2006, p.67.
3 Ibid.
4 Cullen, Lisa Takeuchi, Time Magazine, February 27, 2006, p. 48.

Chapter 10:
1 Gardner, Beth, USA Today
2 Koss-Feder, Laura, "That's Funny!," Time Magazine, December, 2005, pp.F1-F3
3 Ibid.
4 Guroff, Margaret, "Sally Field," AARP, September/October, 2006, p. 68.
5 www.youngatheartchorus.com

Chapter 11:
1 Gibbs, Nancy, Time Magazine, "Midlife Crisis? Bring it on!,"May 16, 2005, pp. 53-63.
2 Robinson, Grady Jim, "The Role of Myth in Speaking," Audio cassette.

Check Out These Websites

www.aarp.org
www.eons.com
www.civicventures.org
www.livingto100.com
www.myboomerang.org
www.thetransitionnetwork.org
www.pathwaysmarion.com
www.elderhostel.org
www.ssa.gov/planners/calculators.htm
www.blogster.com
www.joeklock.com
www.sixthstar.com
www.youngatheartchorus.com
www.psfollies.com
www.basketobooks.com
www.prosperousboomer.com
www.spunkyoldbroad.com
www.glennasalsbury.com
www.treasures4teachers.org
www.gorgeousgrandma.com
www.vocationvacations.com

Visit Phyllis's websites:

www.refiredretired.com
BUY "ReFIRED" merchandise there! Great gifts!

www.keystoparadise.info
BUY *Keys to Paradise…a fun guide to Key West!*

www.wingspanconnection.com
Seminars, training
BOOK PHYLLIS FOR YOUR "REFIRED" KEYNOTE!

About Phyllis...

Before Moving to Key West

This was Phyllis May, Ph.D., prior to moving to Key West. Another life...wife, mother, Superintendent of Schools... hair done twice a week, stressed, divorce, daughter off to college, dog put to sleep, mother to assisted living...

RETIRED!

After Moving to Key West

This is Phyllis May after 8 years in Key West. Another life...temp, concierge, student, B&B (sometimes cooked breakfast), fairies' godmother, seminar leader, wedding planner, Poopette (worked at Pelican Poop Shop) and hopeless volunteer/board member/officer for many non-profit organizations.

ReFIRED!!

Photo by Roger Cousineau

Order Form

☐ *Keys to Paradise...a fun guide to Key West* $11.95
☐ *ReFIRED, not Retired* $14.95
SUBTOTAL . . . .$ _____
FL residents add 7.5% sales tax . . . $ _____
12% shipping and handling . . . $ _____
ORDER TOTAL . . . $ _____

Buy both for $20 + tax, s&h

Name _____

Mailing Address _____

City _____ State/Province _____

Country _____ Zip _____

Telephone ( ) _____

Email _____

☐ Author Autograph: Personalize Inscription to read:

_____

_____

Make checks payable to: Keys to Paradise, Inc.

Which credit card will you use?_____

Card # _____

Expiration date _____ CD# on back _____

Keys to Paradise, Inc.
1800 Atlantic Blvd.
A-312
Key West, FL 33040
Phone orders: (305) 295-7501/ tollfree at (877) 312-1800
Fax: (305) 294-7095

Multiple copy prices available

Don't forget...
Chase's Calendar of Events recognizes
March 1

ReFired
NOT **Retired**
Day

Why don't you promote it in you community and let me know what you did? As a charter member of *ReFIRED, not Retired*, you are now an official ambassador to promote it. Go to the website at www.refiredretired.com or contact me at info@refiredretired.com for more information. Spread the word...

REFIRE NOW!

Now, what direction is your deck chair facing?